CREATIVE
Machine
Embroidery

CREATIVE Machine Embroidery

KRISTEN DIBBS

SIMON & SCHUSTER
AUSTRALIA

CREATIVE MACHINE EMBROIDERY

First published in Australasia in 1995 by
Simon & Schuster Australia
20 Barcoo Street, East Roseville NSW 2069

Viacom International
Sydney New York London Toronto Tokyo Singapore

National Library of Australia
Cataloguing-in-Publication data

Dibbs, Kristen.
    Creative machine embroidery.

    Bibliography.
    ISBN 0 7318 0452 X.

    1. Embroidery, Machine. I. Title.

746.44038

Diagrams by Anna Warren
Photography by Joseph Filshie
Designed by Joy Eckermann
Typeset in Australia by Asset Typesetting Pty Ltd
Printed by KHL Printing in Singapore

The publishers wish to thank Joanna Hill, Sara Haddad
and Nicki Robilliard for kindly agreeing to model some
of the garments photographed within this book.

FOREWORD

Do you ever find yourself stuck for a beginning? How to word a foreword, for instance? Kristen Dibbs, author of this fine book, is a constant reminder to me that the way to begin is to play, something she does intelligently and with zest, both in her textile work and in her own way with words. In fact, she now writes a regular column ('Away with words') for the magazine that I edit, *Textile Fibre Forum*.

I also know Kristen in her capacity as a hands-on teacher, and as a maker. I shall never forget the pleasure of modelling a garment named 'Scheherezade's Robe' during our 1994 textile conference. This work of machine-made lace came from the persistent sewing and creative determination of that talented lady and I would love to make it mine forever.

It seems universally agreed that the textile arts need a higher profile — so how does this come about? Start with a method: machine embroidery. Master it. Begin to look for new applications. Find them. Consider the new technologies. Apply them. Look beyond decoration — perhaps toward sculpture; certainly towards mixed media. Share your vision.

I think that not only is Kristen Dibbs a leader in exploring new applications for machine embroidery, she is also a skilled communicator.

It follows that inspiration as well as instruction lies within these pages. You may decide, after studying this book, that making metres of Scheherezade's lacy fabric from slippery rayon ribbon is not precisely for you, but you will certainly find the ideas and projects that are for you. And you will discover the joy and the sheer logic of being taught by Kristen Dibbs.

JANET DE BOER

Janet De Boer is the Executive Director of The Australia Forum for Textile Arts, and is editor of the international magazine Textile Fibre Forum.

CONTENTS

ACKNOWLEDGMENTS

To my husband, Richard, and to my sons, James and Phillip, for love, support and encouragement, and for keeping me in touch with the world outside the sewing room.

To Bernina Australia, especially Michael Orvis, a modern Medici.

To Janet De Boer, and The Australian Forum for Textile Arts, for doing so much to raise the profile and status of textile art throughout Australia.

Thank you all.

INTRODUCTION

Since writing my first book, I've spent a great deal of time travelling in order to teach workshops around Australia. To all of the wonderful people I've met, a sincere thank you, for making me so welcome and for sharing with me your excitement for machine embroidery. Somebody once defined this technique as 'sewing that's meant to be seen', in contrast to more utilitarian applications where the best sewing is invisible and used for joining or neatening fabric.

In recent years, machine embroidery in Australia has blossomed, as increasing numbers of people discover the satisfaction of creating something unique, whether for personal use, exhibition, competition or sale. More and more senior high school students are using textiles to interpret their major works, and many of their pieces are chosen for exhibition with the most successful senior school artworks. This reflects a gratifying level of support from both teachers and parents, who see textiles as an exciting and expressive medium for a huge range of concepts. There has also been an encouraging increase in the number of high-quality textile exhibitions presented in Australia, as the gallery directors see the enormous amount of interest generated by these works. The supreme example of this excitement was a textile exhibition by Annemieke Mein, which was held in Melbourne in 1992. During the six weeks of the exhibition, the exquisite machine embroidery depicting Australian wildlife was seen by over 100,000 people, many of whom queued for over three hours. This rivals the interest in imported major exhibitions by European masters.

Several capital cities now hold festivals, where major displays of embroidery, quilts, art clothing and textiles are shown concurrently. These events are becoming increasingly popular with members of the public, from both Australia and overseas. Residential workshops in many different textile areas are proliferating, and the intensity of interest in them underlines the significance they have for the participants, many of whom have told me it is the first time they have left their spouse, family, farm or business in up to thirty years. It is also deeply satisfying to see the increased level of self-esteem in so many who have discovered how liberating it is to be creative.

I hope that you will enjoy this book, and develop your own style and forms of expression, perhaps using some of the techniques outlined here as a starting point. Feel free to change, combine, interpret and experiment, and revel in the wonderful sense of achievement that comes with creating something that is uniquely yours.

PROJECT KEY

These symbols are used throughout the book.

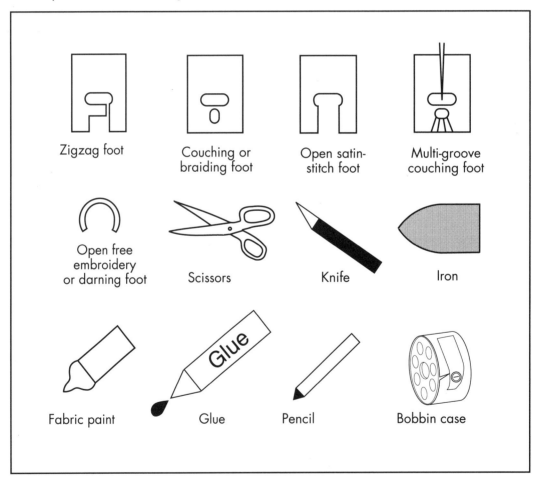

Zigzag foot

Couching or braiding foot

Open satin-stitch foot

Multi-groove couching foot

Open free embroidery or darning foot

Scissors

Knife

Iron

Fabric paint

Glue

Pencil

Bobbin case

PARTS OF A SEWING MACHINE

Illustration supplied by Bernina Australia

1	Stitch plate	12	Needle position knob
2	Presser foot	13	Power switch
3	Pattern indicator	14	Buttonhole knob
4	Pre-tension stud	15	Stitch length knob
5	Thread tension slot	16	Stitch program selection knob
6	Basic setting level	17	Selector knob for sewing/darning
7	Selector lever	18	Presser foot lifter socket
8	Bobbin spindle	19	Carrying handle
9	Engaging lever for bobbin winder	20	Sewing light switch
10	Handwheel	21	Thread guide
11	Stitch width knob	22	Thread holder pins

Some Basic Sewing Hints

Following are some useful techniques which are used in many of the projects in this book, and which are also helpful to remember for all your sewing.

Bringing Up The Bobbin Thread

It is important that you do not leave threads trailing underneath your work as they may become caught in the feed teeth. To avoid this, always begin by bringing the bobbin thread to the surface. Do this by holding the end of the top thread in your left hand while turning the handwheel forward with your right hand so that the needle goes down into the fabric and comes up again to the highest point. (On some machines this may be done by tapping the foot control gently so that the machine sews one stitch.) Pull gently on the top thread so that the lower thread is brought up through the hole in the needle plate and through the fabric.

Anchoring The Thread

To secure the threads ends so that they are not pulled down under the fabric or do not become tangled, hold the ends of the top and bottom threads while making a few small stitches close together over the loose ends. Snip off the thread ends close to the fabric.

Beginning Satin Stitch To Avoid Unravelling

Bring up the bobbin thread. Position the presser foot over the point where the threads come through the fabric. Make several stitches over the thread ends to secure them, and then snip off the thread ends and continue sewing. The thread ends will be secured invisibly under the stitching.

Ending Satin Stitch To Avoid Unravelling

For wide satin stitch Stitch to the end. Use the reverse control to stitch backwards for 5 to 6 stitches. Change the needle position to one side, and the stitch width to zero. Make a few small stitches on the edge of the band of satin stitch so that they blend invisibly. If you are unable to change your needle position, change the stitch width to zero, raise the presser foot and move the fabric slightly so that the needle enters just at the edge of the band of satin stitch. Take a few small straight stitches down the side to the end of the satin stitch. Snip off the thread ends or pull them through to the back with a hand needle and darn them in.

For tapered satin stitch Make a few tiny stitches at the point and snip off the threads or darn them in by hand.

COVERING ENDS OF COUCHED THREADS OR YARNS

Couched yarn ends can be covered and secured in a number of ways:

1. Begin and end all couched yarns in the seam allowance so that they will be caught in the seam.

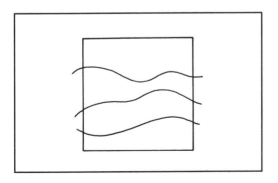

2. Cover the end of the couched yarn with a small length of satin stitch that tapers to a point at the end of the yarn. Use an embroidery thread that matches the yarn. To cover the beginning of the yarn, finish the couching, then go back and cover the starting end in the same way. This is the best method for thick yarn or cord.

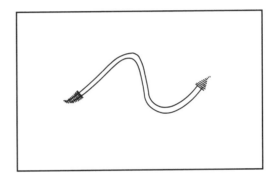

3. Tuck the ends of couched yarns under folds and pleats of fabric, or under a piece of appliquéd fabric.

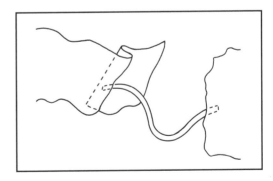

4. Fold over 1 cm ($\frac{1}{2}$ in.) length of yarn at each end and start and finish by stitching over this double

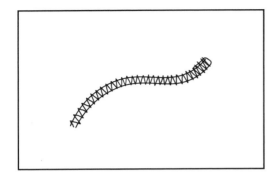

USING PAPER-BACKED FUSIBLE WEBBING

For any activities involving fusible webbing, use baking paper under and over the fusible material to avoid getting glue on the iron or ironing board. If you get glue on the iron, use commercial hot-iron cleaner (found in supermarkets). This is squeezed onto towelling, and the hot iron-plate scrubbed to remove the mess. Non-stick irons can simply be wiped clean with a soft cloth. Glue residue can sometimes be removed from the fabric with methylated spirits. Test it on a sample of fabric first.

thickness. This works well with finer yarns where a double thickness will not be too bulky.

MITRING CORNERS

For a neat finish on an article with fabric folded to the wrong side, e.g. on belts and bags, fold and press the long sides over (*fig. 1*). Fold each corner of the short side down to form a triangular fold, press, and then fold over the short end (*fig. 2*). The triangular fold will point directly to the corner, avoiding the bulk along the edge (*fig. 3*).

STRETCHING THE FABRIC IN A HOOP

Check that the two hoops fit together snugly and that the inner hoop is wrapped with bias binding. Thicker fabric will require a looser fit. Place the outside hoop on the

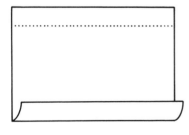

Fig. 1

Fig. 2

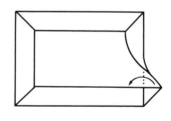

Fig. 3

table and spread the fabric over it, right side up. Stand up and lean over the hoop to press the inner hoop into position while stretching the fabric so that it is stretched tightly. Sometimes, with delicate fabrics which cannot be stretched further when in the hoop, you can tape or pin each corner of the fabric to the table, to hold them taut while you press the inner hoop into place. Remove the tape or pins. Tug the fabric gently and tighten the screw further to achieve the necessary drum-like tightness of the fabric.

LOOSENING THE TOP TENSION

This is suggested in many projects to prevent the bobbin thread from showing, or to prevent fine thread from breaking. First establish where normal tension is on your machine. Check your machine manual and make a note of the number or setting. A lower number generally means a looser tension. (Remember the two 'Ls' — lower/looser.) If you have a plus or minus sign for top tension, the minus sign stands for looser tension. Only loosen the tension when it is required, and return it to normal afterwards.

On some machines, it is possible to slightly tighten the lower tension by threading the bobbin thread through a small hole in the finger of the bobbin. This is often recommended for sewing buttonholes and may be sufficient to stop the bobbin thread from showing.

TROUBLESHOOTING

When you are coming to grips with a new technique, or doing experimental work, you will encounter new problems. If something goes wrong, first check your machine handbook to make sure that you are using the machine correctly (machine threaded properly, bobbin wound and inserted the right way, etc.). Quite often I meet students who have been using their machines for years and are still using very odd methods of bobbin winding or machine threading, then wondering why they have problems.

One student had constant problems with her machine's tension, and her bobbins looked like birds' nests. When I asked her to show me how she wound them, I was amazed at the system she had derived. I asked her why, and she replied that she always used that method. I asked her what the instructions in the book showed, and she replied in surprise, 'Oh, would that be in the book?' The moral of that story is: learn about your machine from the people who made it. READ THE INSTRUCTIONS FIRST. For instructions specific to your machine and machine embroidery, refer to the books by Jackie Dodson, *Know Your Sewing Machine*. They are published by Chilton and are available for all major brands.

To keep your machine in top working condition, it is a good idea to book it in for an annual service and check-up. It is unrealistic to expect any appliances to perform well without regular maintenance. Some people are surprised when their machine gives up after an intensive morning's sewing in a workshop. Would you expect anyone to perform well in a marathon if they had only been training by taking a weekly jog around the block?

One of the most annoying problems encountered by machine service departments stems from customers who complain about problems as soon as their machine is returned. Check all your basic functions when you get your machine back, and make sure you have turned all the correct switches and dials to the 'on' position before ringing for service. Check your machine manual for detailed instructions about setting up the machine for sewing. This information was given to me by a service man from a leading company who is often called out by customers complaining that the machine won't go after returning from service, usually because the switch on the machine had not been turned on!

SOME COMMON PROBLEMS

Needle breaks

If your needle breaks it is a nerve-racking experience, although safety glasses make it less of a hazard. In any case, stop, remove the broken needle and brush out the bobbin area to remove any tiny needle fragments which may damage your machine. Always replace the new needle tightly and correctly.

Solutions

- The needle may be the wrong size for machine embroidery. Sizes 80 and 90 are good to work with as very fine needles break more easily, and very heavy needles such as size 110 are almost as thick as the slit in the needle plate, giving you little leeway for error.
- You may be moving the hoop too fast and jerking it, and/or sewing too slowly and pulling on the needle. Sew at a steady speed and move the hoop slowly.
- There may be too many folds or thicknesses of fabric for the needle to pass through. Rearrange the fabric, and don't make multiple thicknesses of anything tough or dense.
- The feed teeth cover plate may

have slipped. Check and replace.
- You may have sewn over an area too thick for the needle, e.g. the edge of a satin-stitched hole in cutwork, or over a machine-embroidered bead. Leave very intense close stitching until last.
- The spool of thread may have been jerked and spun backwards, wrapping the thread around the spool pin. Try to gradually build up speed as you begin sewing.
- The machine foot may have been loosened by intensive sewing. Check and retighten.
- The needle may not be inserted correctly, or the needle clamp may not have been tightened sufficiently. Check and retighten.
- If you are using a walking foot, a ruffler, or any attachment that fits around the screw holding the needle in position, check the tightness of the screw regularly as prolonged use can loosen it, causing the needle to fall out.
- *Never* attempt to sharpen a needle by sewing through sandpaper. This is a myth. If the needle is blunt, throw it away and use a new one.

Top thread breaks or shreds

Solutions

- Top tension may be too tight. Loosen slightly.
- Embroidery thread performs better through a needle with a

large eye and with loosened top tension.

- The thread may be old and/or dry. Place it in a plastic bag in the refrigerator overnight.
- Thread may be poor quality. Buy only good quality brand name thread and keep it in a covered box away from dust and to prevent it from drying out.
- The machine or bobbin may be incorrectly threaded. Check and rethread.
- The thread fibres may be caught in the tension disc. Pull a length of thread carefully through the disc to dislodge any scraps.
- The top thread may have wound itself around the spool spin. Cover the spool with a length of tubular finger bandage and push it down to the bottom of the spool when in use. Alternatively, use a thread guide to keep the thread from falling down the spool. In an emergency, make your own thread guide from a large-eyed darning needle taped to the back of the machine.
- Sometimes a needle may have a slight irregularity in the eye, or a rough spot which shreds the thread. Change to a new needle.

Bobbin thread breaks

Solutions
- The bottom tension may be too

tight. Check your machine's instruction manual.
- The bobbin may be unevenly wound. Check your machine's manual for the correct winding procedure. Do not wind bobbins over leftover threads. For even tension, always wind onto an empty bobbin and wind at a medium speed.
- The bobbin thread may have slipped out of the bobbin tension spring. Check and replace.

Thread looping and tangling underneath

Solutions
- This is usually the result of no top tension. Clean out the tangle of threads and lower the presser foot lever before sewing to engage the tension.
- Check that the top thread has not slipped out of the guide leading into the tension disc. This happens with some brands when sewing at high speeds.

Stitches not forming properly

Solutions
- If you are sewing without a hoop, the fabric may be riding up the needle and therefore the threads may not be looping properly underneath. Stretch the fabric in a hoop.
- If you are sewing without a foot, the same thing may happen. Use a darning foot. If you have variable

pressure, increase the pressure on the foot enough to hold the fabric down while still allowing it to move freely.

- The fabric may not be stretched tightly enough in the hoop. Check and retighten.
- The needle may not be inserted high enough in the needle clamp. Push it up as far as it will go before tightening the screw. Check that the needle is the right way round, and that you are using the correct needle system for your machine.
- Some sewing machines require a particular type of needle for successful free machine embroidery. Check this with your machine dealer.
- Some older machines perform beautifully for ordinary sewing, but sulk if the feed teeth are lowered. Check with your machine dealer if your machine persistently refuses to do free machine embroidery.

Fabric not moving or moving unevenly through machine

Solutions
- Check that the feed teeth are raised. (This is a common problem with beginners.) When the feed teeth lever is changed to the up position, the teeth may not pop straight up, but will move up with the first stitch taken.

- If the fabric is moving unevenly or to one side, the feed teeth may be clogged with matted threads. Clean out the area with a brush. Lubricate the area if necessary.

Needle makes a plopping sound or plucks at the fabric

Solutions
- The needle may be blunt or the point bent. Use a new needle.
- On cotton buckram, plastic or paper, the needle may make a plopping noise as it punches a hole in the solid surface. Make sure you use fresh, sharp, strong needles.

Shakes, rattles and ominous noises

Solutions
- Stop sewing. Check to see if anything is obviously loose, e.g. if the bobbin case has been inserted incorrectly, the foot not tightened, the needle plate not made secure, or if the sewing extension table has been incorrectly attached. Next, check if anything has dropped into the machine, e.g. screws from machine feet, broken needle fragments, and so on. Clean and oil the machine. Check again, turning the handwheel to see if the noise reoccurs. If the machine is still noisy or is making new and unfamiliar sounds, stop sewing and have it serviced. Sewing with a problem can cost you more money in repairs.

FIBRE SPEAK

It is often thought that artists whose work is in print or in galleries spend their days cranking out masterpieces while sheltering in an ivory tower. In real life, they are probably battling away at the kitchen sink/ supermarket/kindergarten/second job just like normal people. Yet when you read about them and their work in the latest art/craft journal, it is often difficult to understand what is being discussed, because much of what we see printed on expensive paper is couched in terms that few can understand. (Sometimes I suspect that even the artist is often surprised to read obscure opinions attributed to them, but expressed in terms that nobody would ever believe they had uttered. After all, *they* don't even talk like that!)

However, there are some phrases that, cunningly but casually inserted into your conversation, may present you, too, as a well-organised professional. They are as follows:

Work in progress It isn't finished yet, but the photos submitted in your application prove that work is proceeding on *something*. The title of the unfinished work, 'Cosmic Negativism III', may mean that the artist is leaving lots of leeway in case the completed work changes direction en route.

Organic forms Shapes used in the work that resemble unidentifiable living forms, and indicate that the artist is deeply concerned with life, growth and the environment.

Working intuitively Making it up; playing by ear. Many textile artists (this author included) begin by playing sensuously with their fabric collection, and developing any subsequent inspiration. To some, this seems less worthy than working on intricately detailed plans, drawings and preordained concepts. However, those who belong to the intuitive school often find that by the time the plans are drawn and the diagrams detailed, the freshness has gone out of the idea and they are anxious to move on to something else.

Manipulating textiles Another way of saying you are playing with the fabric collection, often as the first step in the creative process. It also involves bending, folding, twisting, knotting, tearing, ruching, ruffling, plaiting, smocking, pleating and so on, in an effort to make the surface more exciting.

Creative block No ideas or desire to create. This condition sometimes has a domestic advantage, as normally repellent chores, like an encrusted oven or the inaccessible sludge under the sink, are enthusiastically tackled in an effort to avoid resolving the current textile problem. Often happens as a direct result of a **deadline.**

Deadline Date circled on calendar, preceded by not nearly enough days to complete the work. The days leading up to a deadline are those most likely to be filled with unexpected domestic dramas, e.g. chicken pox, uninvited house guests, appliance breakdowns or marital strife.

Fragment Small piece of work with unfinished edges; presented as precious. Sometimes a large piece that lacks charisma can be successfully recycled into several smaller fragments. These can then be presented as a **series.**

Series Several works with the same theme, usually using the same media, and possibly originating from the same piece. This is also a good way to get additional mileage out of one bright idea.

Studio The inadequate portion of the family room available for creative work, usually shared with ironing board, video, TV and several teenagers and/or cats.

Garagio Variation of studio, but shared with assorted car, boat and lawn mower spare parts, half empty paint tins and long-term repair projects relating to spouse's work in progress.

Resource collection Ten years accumulation of magazines, newspaper articles, books and clippings which will be organised and catalogued when there is space available in life and **studio** to do this.

Materials collection The contents of several tea chests, many cardboard cartons, three cupboards and the sagging space in the top of the wardrobe, as well as four Hong Kong shoppers and the unexplored area behind the laundry where most of the fabric stash has spread to. Family cats love the **materials collection** and often use these areas for sleeping or giving birth, resulting in even more fibrous additions to the surface.

Supportive environment In cases of dire emergency, if an artist's urgent request is supported by either a doctor's certificate or a demand notice from the publisher, the family will cook their own dinner or wash their own socks.

Streamlining operations Teaching the family how to operate can opener, microwave, dishwasher and washing machine. Programming the dial-a-pizza number in the phone memory.

Focusing on the task in hand Ear plugs in the ears while concentrating on the computer or the sewing machine, and ignoring cries of hunger/thirst/sexual frustration from family members. Also applies to the useful acquired skill of **tunnel vision,** which allows one to walk from the bedroom to the **studio,** while ignoring distractions in the kitchen sink or laundry basket.

Inspirational material Large accumulation of natural objects, such as snake skins, fungus, bark, shells, sponges, seed pods, bones, scales, rocks, pebbles, geological specimens, dead beetles, fossils, feathers, dried leaves and driftwood, which overflow their allotted space and which, in case of flood or fire, should be rescued simultaneously with kids, spouse and cats.

Allocating priorities The bathroom/ laundry/kitchen/bedroom is about to be declared a 'toxic waste zone', but if this manuscript isn't finished today, a mortgage will need to be raised on the kids and the publisher's advance refunded.

Protecting your interests Learning to say 'No', and meaning it, when asked to pay bills, collect dry-cleaning, deliver lost property, arrange car servicing or buy socks, underwear, more cereal, bread, soft drink or beer in any other time slot than the once-weekly smash raid on the supermarket and shopping centre.

Title What the work is called so it sounds good in the application or catalogue. Obscure titles (see **Work in progress**) are a real bonus. Intellectuals will compete to interpret the artist's concept.

Evolving work It's developing and changing, and appears to have a life of its own. The subject matter is unclear, but hopefully a **title** may soon be suggested. May also refer to a chequered past in fibre, where the artist has moved from macramé, through crochet, lacemaking and weaving, and is now doing meaningful research into the possibilities of origami with corrugated cardboard. Someone will eventually trace these significant steps and point out how purposeful the evolution really was.

Opportunism A gift to the artist of a trailer load of unwanted materials, e.g. fabric scraps (following an attic clearance) or basket-making materials (after razing a backyard jungle). The opportunity is to use this stuff to create saleable artwork or it will have to be palmed off onto another textile artist.

Eclectic Expressive work utilising

lots of bits and pieces, or influences from all over the place, some of which may relate to each other. The current vogue for multimedia eclecticism may soon lead to a craze for hand-embroidered raku-fired cast paper, or double reverse-strand tabby weave barbed wire felting. Or worse.

Ubiquitous Seen everywhere. There's a lot of it going around (like a virus). What was originally an innovative or traditional idea or art form is now presented in a downmarket idiot-proof kit form, meaning that anyone can produce a bastardised form of instant, easy, totally talent-and-skill-free Sashiko — just stamp your dotted white lines, then wear.

Grant Free money given to other people who specialise in the intricate art form of writing really good grant applications.

Functional What it's for. The public, on the whole, prefer art/craft work to be functional, or at least representational. This value is instilled from a very early age, as the two most common questions from parents to their offspring are: 'Beautiful, darling. What is it?' and 'It's lovely, dear. What's it for?' Few kids have the confidence to say, 'It isn't *for* anything, it just is.'

This article was originally published in Textile Fibre Forum *magazine, 1994.*

GUIDELINES FOR TEXTILES

During the past few years, I've worked with many secondary and tertiary students in both art and textile classes. One of the topics most often discussed concerns how to go about making a major work in textiles. Frequently, students pursue an idea because it's the only one they've got — not because it's the best idea of many ideas considered. To help you discover the best idea for a work, and to help you determine how to produce that work, this section reveals the things you should consider before making any final decisions.

These lists were developed after numerous brainstorming sessions with many artists and students. They are not exhaustive lists — I'm sure that just reading them will suggest other considerations to you. Write them in the margins of this book — it's meant to be used. Also, it may be a good idea to make a copy of the list so that you can use it to tick off each relevant question every time you are considering a new work.

Some of the lists overlap, as design or technique decisions tend to flow in many different directions. The primary aims of the whole process are to make your final choice as well informed as possible and to avoid being frustrated halfway through a project because of an unforeseen difficulty.

I know some artists prefer to work intuitively (I'm one of them!), but even so, I have learned the hard way to give serious thought to many of the aspects mentioned here before I begin playing with my fabrics and working towards a final design. When constraints of time and money affect a project, I can't afford to jump in head first and then discover that the work can't be properly displayed, delivered on time, sold for a profit or fulfil the competition guidelines without a dramatic change of direction. The temptation is always to begin with the most familiar or enjoyable part of a project, and then discover later that doing so presents a problem of finishing or assembly.

Sometimes it helps to make out a checklist, noting time, interim deadlines for photography, application submission and so on, and listing the processes required after making initial trials or samplers. Samplers of techniques on different materials may pinpoint difficulties early, thus avoiding panics or expensive mistakes. Preliminary experiments like

Above: *Denim skirt with fast patches* (page 36), *twin-needled vest* (page 65) *and raffia hat with ribbon lace flowers* (page 46)

Above: *Bedjacket made with quilted scrap patches* (page 70)

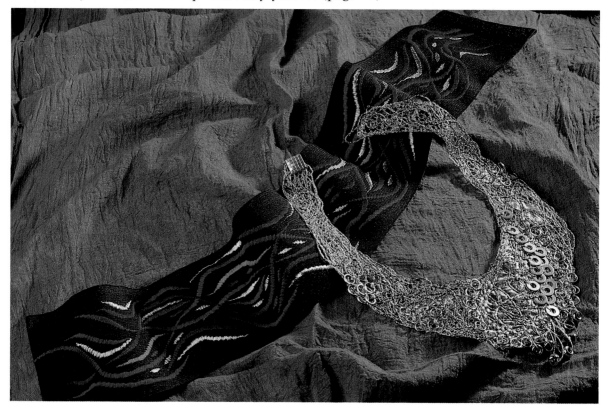

Above: *Gold necklace* (page 77) *and embroidered elastic* (page 39)

these will also help you estimate more accurately the time required for a particular project.

Some suggestions here relate to professional work, but don't feel that every time you sit down to make something you need to ask yourself 200 questions and make a flow chart. After all, how hard can it be to sew six pot holders for the fête? Just bear in mind the areas to be considered when beginning a major work in textiles.

WHY?

What is the main reason for making this work?
- ❏ Examination requirements
- ❏ Competition
- ❏ Commission
- ❏ Exhibition
- ❏ Demonstration of skill
- ❏ Sale
- ❏ Gift
- ❏ Personal wardrobe or display
- ❏ Experimentation
- ❏ Practice
- ❏ Utilising special materials
- ❏ Recycling existing materials
- ❏ Recreation
- ❏ Relaxation
- ❏ Creative expression
- ❏ Personal statement of concern (e.g. environmental preservation)

WHEN?
- ❏ How much time is available for this project?
- ❏ hours
- ❏ days
- ❏ weeks
- ❏ months
- ❏ Can all available time be spent on this or will other projects be proceeding simultaneously?
- ❏ Will there be interim deadlines for examination assessment or for presentation of slides and photos to accompany entry forms for exhibitions or competitions?
- ❏ Does work need to meet an earlier deadline to allow for framing or transport?
- ❏ What time has been allowed for contingencies?
- ❏ Have samples or trials been done to more accurately estimate time for quotations, pricing and so on?

BUDGET
- ❏ How much money is available for this project?
- ❏ Whose money is it?
- ❏ Will it be available before the project is commenced or only when it is finished?
- ❏ Does an estimate of cost of materials and/or labour need to be submitted before or after the project?
- ❏ For a commissioned piece, is a deposit required before the project commences, and is it refundable?
- ❏ If the work is to be sold for profit, what other expenses should be considered (such as entry fees, transport costs, display material, presentation, insurance, photography, labels, publicity)?

❑ If the work is to be sent on consignment, how is the commission to be calculated on the sale price of the work?

TRANSPORT

❑ How will the work be transported?

❑ Does it need to fit a certain size container or package for delivery?

❑ Will the packaging affect the work in any way (e.g. crushing or breakage), or can the work be designed to be more easily transportable?

❑ How will the work be returned?

❑ Is advance booking required for transport?

❑ Are any special packing materials or containers required?

❑ If the work is to travel overseas, are there any restrictions on the materials used (e.g. feathers, skins, etc.)?

DISPLAY

❑ How should the work be presented?
  ❑ on a wall
  ❑ on a body or a mannequin
  ❑ as a mobile
  ❑ as a free-standing sculpture

❑ Does any special display material or special instructions for display need to be submitted with the work?

❑ Does the artist have any control over the way the work will be presented?

❑ How will the work be viewed — from a distance or close-up, and from what angle?

❑ Will the work be inspected both inside and out?

❑ Will the work be handled by others?

❑ If so, will it withstand this?

❑ Will the display be static or will the work be presented in a performance?

❑ Are special models or dancers required to display the work?

❑ Are any other materials necessary for display (e.g. accessories, hanging materials, lighting)?

❑ Are any special labels or signs required?

❑ Can the display space that is to be used or the area where the commissioned work is to be placed be inspected beforehand?

❑ If not, are photographs available of this area?

TECHNIQUES

❑ Are any special techniques required for this work?

❑ Do these need to be learned or practised?

❑ Does the artist have sufficient skill in this technique to complete the work successfully?

❑ Will the chosen techniques be appropriate for the time allowed to complete the work?

❑ Is the technique cost effective if the work is primarily intended for sale?

❑ If the work is to be inspected closely, how good does the finish need to be?

❑ If the work is to be viewed from a distance, will small intricate details be visible?

❑ If the work is intended for competition or assessment, does the technique need any further explanation as to the skills involved?

❑ How important are innovative techniques for the purpose of the work?

❑ Is the technique suitable for the design and/or materials chosen?

❑ If several techniques are involved, in which order should these be done?

❑ Will the most difficult and time-consuming technique be the most effective?

❑ Have several techniques been tried to determine the best one to interpret the design, taking into consideration the time, budget and display requirements of the work?

MATERIALS

❑ Are the materials compatible with the chosen technique and design, and with other materials within the design?

❑ Do the materials enhance the chosen design or dominate it?

❑ Are these materials easy to work with?

❑ What other materials would also achieve the same result?

❑ Can unusual materials be combined with a traditional technique (or vice versa) for an innovative result?

❑ Are sufficient materials available to allow for practice, experimentation and mistakes?

❑ Are there any restrictions on use, type or quantity of materials?

❑ Have samples been made to estimate the quantity of materials required?

❑ Are the chosen materials compatible with the budget?

❑ Are they readily available or do they need to be ordered in advance?

❑ Will materials need to be purchased, collected or recycled?

❑ Do the required materials need any treatment before use (e.g. dyeing, cleaning, preshrinking)?

❑ Are there any special requirements for the materials (e.g. colourfast, non-toxic, shrinkproof, fire-resistant, waterproof, made of natural fibres, handmade from fibre by the artist, etc.)?

❑ Are any special safety requirements necessary when working with these materials (e.g. protective clothing or masks when using dyes, solvents, etc.)?

❑ Are materials perishable or fragile?

❑ Do any of them have a shelf-life?

❑ Has this been checked before purchase to ensure freshness?

❑ Will these materials require any special storage (e.g. low humidity, flat storage, low-light storage, extra clean or dust free, rolled, folded, boxed or hung)?

❑ Is space available for this?

❑ Is there any special equipment required for using these materials (e.g. special machine accessories, feet or needles, larger tables to support the materials, any other hardware or software)?

❑ Will the chosen materials react well to transport or packing?

❑ Do they crush easily?

❑ How long will the work be required to last and under what conditions?

❑ Are any special cleaning and/or preservation techniques required?

SIZE

❑ What size should the work be?

❑ Are there any restrictions of size regarding display or transport?

❑ Is the size appropriate for the purpose of the work?

❑ Are multiple sizes or a particular size required?

❑ Are any special fittings or measurements needed before choosing a size?

❑ Can a large work be divided into smaller areas then reassembled?

❑ Will it be easier to work in small modules or larger shapes?

❑ Is the work area suitable for making a very large piece?

INSPIRATION

❑ What is needed in the way of inspirational material or information before commencing the work?

❑ Photographs of specific materials from books or field trips

❑ Actual examples or specimens from field trips or excursions

❑ Reference drawings from specimens, museums or art galleries

❑ Historical references from libraries, science museums, textile collections, videos or films

❑ Slides of submitted work from previous exhibitions

❑ The Australian Forum for Textile Arts (TAFTA) slide collections, or artwork and techniques

❑ Videos of fashion parades

❑ Exhibitions of particular interest or similar themes

❑ Art, craft and fashion magazines

Information can also be obtained from specific group collections, e.g. Embroiderers' Guild, Lace Makers' Guild, Costume and Textile Society, Quilters' Guild, Powerhouse Museum archives, crafts councils and art galleries.

CONTRACTS AND LEGALITIES

❑ Is it necessary to have a contract drawn up before work commences?

❑ Are the requirements and specifications clearly stated?

❑ How binding is the contract?

❑ How can it be enforced?

❑ What are the individual's responsibilities regarding the contract?

❑ What contingencies does it cover?

❑ Are the terms of payments, deposit and so on clearly stated?

❑ If the work is commissioned, does the client have a right to refuse the completed work?

❑ If the work is to be sold on consignment, what arrangements have been made about insurance, commission on sales and return of unsold work?

❑ What insurance is necessary for the work while in transit or on display?

❑ Who is responsible for this?

❑ Are these details in writing?

DESIGN

❑ Does the design have a particular theme or concept?

❑ Whose design will be used for the piece?

❑ If you are working to another's design, who has the final decision?

❏ How many designs need to be submitted for a client to choose from?

❏ How much leeway does the artist have in interpreting a client's design?

❏ Will commercial patterns be used or should the design be original? (Some commercial patterns have stringent restrictions on display or resale.)

❏ Is the design compatible with the materials and techniques chosen?

❏ Will it withstand normal wear and cleaning techniques?

❏ Can the design be simplified to enhance the technique or materials?

❏ Does the design need to be traditional, conventional, experimental, innovative or outrageous?

SHAPES

POSITIVE SHAPES

There are many way to create positive shapes in your chosen design. These include the techniques of:

❏ appliquéd fabric

❏ insets of contrasting colour, texture, tone, fabric, technique. (Alternatively, you can contrast the background with these techniques, e.g. by overlaying sheer fabric on the shape or background for contrast.)

❏ silk-screen printing

❏ fabric painting

❏ silk painting

❏ shadow embroidery

❏ making up areas of attached objects, e.g. buttons, beads, sequins, feathers, felt, lace, crochet motifs, torn shapes, glue,

paper, natural fibres, grass, raffia, bark, twigs and found objects, etc.

Some other techniques include:

❏ stitching and stuffing shapes

❏ quilting or using cornelli embroidery around the background of shapes

❏ using concentric lines to form a shape

NEGATIVE SHAPES

This list includes ways of forming a hole or the space of a specific shape. Techniques to use are:

❏ cutting holes

❏ cutwork

❏ burning holes with flame

❏ melting holes with a chemical, e.g. acetone

❏ dissolving holes in soluble fabric

❏ pushing threads aside to form a hole

❏ punching or perforating fabric

❏ tearing holes

❏ making a border or frame around a space

❏ cutting away or drawing threads from a fabric shape

❏ laying lines over open space to form smaller shapes

LINES

Ways of making lines in or on textiles include:

❏ stitched lines

❏ seams

❏ creases

❏ folds

❏ tucks

❏ pleats

❏ pintucks

- ❏ twin-needling
- ❏ couched threads or yarns
- ❏ appliquéd fabric strips
- ❏ appliquéd objects arranged in lines
- ❏ woven areas
- ❏ lines of holes
- ❏ zippers
- ❏ buttonholes in lines
- ❏ threaded ribbon
- ❏ crochet
- ❏ applied braid or lace
- ❏ inset areas of contrasting fabric
- ❏ ruched strips
- ❏ fringing
- ❏ frills and ruffles
- ❏ feathers
- ❏ wire and plastic
- ❏ ribbing on knits
- ❏ woven ridges
- ❏ lines of resist on dyed fabric
- ❏ trapunto (stuffed channels on fabric)
- ❏ quilting
- ❏ positive shapes arranged in lines
- ❏ negative shapes arranged in lines
- ❏ hems
- ❏ frayed edges
- ❏ tears
- ❏ elastic gathered lines
- ❏ applied or inset lines of contrasting tone
- ❏ texture or colour
- ❏ drawn threads
- ❏ multi-layered hems
- ❏ overlocking or flatlocking

- ❏ stamping or impressing
- ❏ lines of fabric paint
- ❏ silk-screened or painted lines
- ❏ cording

TEXTURE

Ways of changing the surface of the textile include:

- ❏ manipulating the surface by rolling, crushing, crumpling, creasing, folding, bending, curving, etc.
- ❏ melting or heatshrinking
- ❏ dissolving areas
- ❏ stitching in lines
- ❏ automatic patterns
- ❏ stitching with thick threads
- ❏ couching cord, yarn, string, ribbon or raffia
- ❏ gathering
- ❏ smocker pleating
- ❏ felting
- ❏ compressing
- ❏ impressing
- ❏ stamping
- ❏ perforating
- ❏ punching holes
- ❏ steel brushing
- ❏ sandpapering
- ❏ scorching
- ❏ cutting and weaving
- ❏ external seams
- ❏ shaving or clipping pile on a surface, e.g. velvet

CREATIVE MACHINE EMBROIDERY

PROJECTS AND TECHNIQUES

EMBROIDERED DENIM PENCIL CASE

Denim has been a fashion classic for decades. It is a wonderful fabric to use for embroidery, especially for beginners, because it is firm enough to work on easily and is also inexpensive. Patterned denim can be used for accents on garments, including collars, pockets, patches, yokes and cuffs. Denim in different colours can be mixed and matched, strip pieced and interspersed with plain fabric. Denim embroidered with white stitching is reminiscent of the traditional Japanese art of *sashiko*, and it is this style that is used in the pencil case described here and shown on page 44.

Always embroider the pattern onto the piece before cutting the fabric out to the correct size, as intensive embroidery may distort the fabric. Also, denim should always be prewashed and ironed before embroidering.

Being the mother of two teenage sons, denim is a favourite fabric for home-made tote bags, pencil cases, drum stick holders, spear gun carriers, book bags and so on, which all look suitably masculine. I'm never allowed to embroider anything other than my sons' names, however, and they spend class time decorating their articles with an amazing variety of graffiti.

I've also made cases for cheque and deposit books for my handbag, and holders for travel documents, air tickets and so on. Check the size of documents and make the case big enough to include a pen or pencil.

MATERIALS

Heavyweight denim fabric, prewashed and ironed
Machine thread, white and colour to match denim
Denim needle, size 90
Zigzag foot
Fabric marking pencil
Ruler
Velcro

METHOD

1. Mark out a piece of denim 28 cm long x 26 cm wide (11 in. x 10 in.). Cut out the fabric to 30 cm long x 28 cm wide (12 in. x 11 in.), thus allowing a 2 cm (1 in.) border around the edge in case the fabric distorts when embroidered. Now mark several vertical guidelines along the 28 cm (11 in.) length to keep pattern straight (see diagram below).

2. Thread the machine with white thread, top and bobbin, using the

denim needle. Set the tension to normal and attach the zigzag foot. Select pattern stitches based on running stitch and sew several close rows of pattern stitches down the length of the fabric using marked guidelines. Several close rows of the same pattern look very effective, whether or not the patterns match. You may also leave open areas of plain fabric.

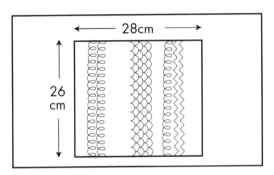

3 Iron the fabric from the wrong side, then trim it to measure 28 cm x 26 cm (11 in. x 10 in.). Overcast or overlock the raw edges. Turn 1 cm ($1/2$ in.) of fabric along the top and bottom edges to the wrong side and iron in place. Cut a strip of Velcro 21 cm ($8^{1}/4$ in.) long, and sew each half of the strip to each end of the fabric,

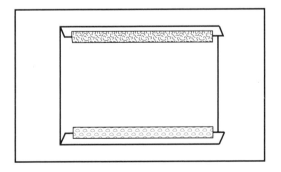

placing the overcast edge of fabric under the Velcro strip (see diagram). Do not sew Velcro in the side seam allowances, as it will be too thick to stitch through. Thread the machine top and bobbin with a colour that matches the denim.

4 Fold the case in half, right sides together, and sew 1 cm ($1/2$ in.) side seams.

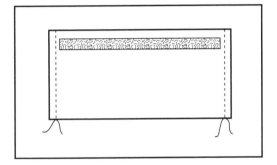

5 Turn the pencil case right side out. Trim the corners and push into shape, then iron. Do not iron over the Velcro as it will melt.

6 Sew another row of stitching down each side of the case, 1 cm ($1/2$ in.) from the edge, securing with extra forwards and backwards stitching at each end.

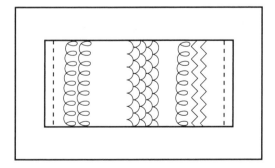

FAST PATCHES – DENIM SKIRT

The very first thing I teach my students (after showing them how to clean and oil their machines) is the versatile technique of sewing forwards and backwards. Five minutes practice on a piece of scrap fabric and any beginner should feel confident enough to try this simple appliqué technique. The best backing fabric to use is a firm even-weave cotton. If the fabric is stiff, e.g. denim, it will not need any further stabilising.

If you wish to use a lighter weight fabric, it is best to stretch each appliqué area in a wooden machine embroidery hoop to prevent the backing fabric from being distorted by the intensive stitching. Stabiliser used behind the fabric is not suitable for this technique as it is almost impossible to remove all the stabiliser afterwards, leaving the fabric undesirably stiff.

Patching is a good survival technique to teach the male members of your family, so they can patch their jeans all by themselves, hopefully leaving you more time to spend on your art appreciation or French conversation classes.

Following is an uncomplicated pattern for a simple, circular, elastic-waisted skirt (shown on page 25).

Alternatively, make or decorate something flat such as a cushion cover or a tote bag.

MATERIALS

Even-weave cotton backing fabric, or denim
Scraps of brightly coloured fabric for appliqué
Wide decorative waistband elastic
Paper-backed fusible webbing
Brightly coloured machine threads
Machine needle, size 80
Zigzag foot
Wooden machine embroidery hoop

METHOD

1 Prewash and iron fabrics. Trace garment pattern onto backing fabric, and cut out 5 cm (2 in.) outside tracing line. The skirt in the picture on page 25 is a full circular flare, cut from 1 square metre of fabric.

2 Place paper-backed fusible webbing glue-side down on the wrong side of the appliqué fabric, and press with a hot iron until fused. Trace and cut out appliqué patches, making sure that each patch is on the true bias of the fabric. You can do this by aligning a diagonal line across each patch with the straight grain of the fabric as shown. This will prevent fraying. The patches used on the skirt in the picture are 5 cm (2 in.) square.

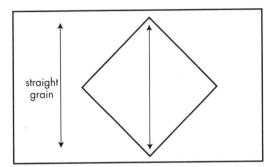

3 Spread the backing fabric on the table and arrange the appliqué pieces on the fabric, making sure that each piece is at least 5 cm (2 in.) away from hems, seams or other patches. When you are satisfied with your arrangement, peel off the backing paper and iron each patch until fused to the backing fabric.

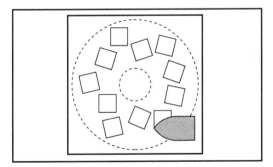

4 Thread the machine with a brightly coloured top thread, and put a colour to match the backing fabric in the bobbin. Loosen the top tension slightly so that the bobbin thread does not show. Attach the zigzag foot and set the stitch length to medium and the stitch width to zero. If you are using a soft backing fabric, stretch the area to be embroidered in an embroidery hoop, and place under the needle before attaching the foot. Place the fabric under the foot, beginning at the corner of one of the patches. Bring the bobbin thread up through the fabric by turning the handwheel, lower the presser foot and take a few stitches to attach the thread. Cut off the thread ends.

5 Sew the first row of stitches down the side of the patch right on the edge. Sew past the edge of the patch for approximately 1 cm (1/2 in.), then press your manual reverse button and sew backwards up the patch, a few millimetres away from your first row, finishing 1 cm (1/2 in.) past the edge of the appliqué fabric. Continue sewing up and down the patch until it is covered with lines of stitching, finishing at a corner.

6 Raise the presser foot lever and turn the fabric, so you can sew more rows of stitching at right angles to the first. As you practise, you will be

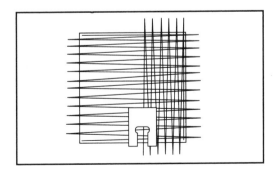

able to sew backwards and forwards without stopping, using your left hand to steer the fabric and keeping your right hand ready to operate the manual reverse button. Make sure you have a line of stitching very close to the edge of each patch. The bias cut edges of each patch will fluff slightly with washing, but the patch will not unravel. Finish the stitching on each patch with a few close straight stitches.

7 Repeat this process for each patch, changing colours as desired. When completed, trim threads

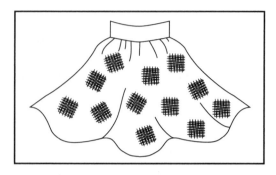

and iron fabric from the wrong side. Replace the garment pattern piece and retrace if necessary. Cut out and make up garment, attaching wide decorative elastic at the waistband.

EMBROIDERED ELASTIC

Embroidered elastic was something I happened upon quite recently. I've been putting all sorts of patterns on ribbons for many years, and extending the idea for use on a high-stretch fabric was an exciting development. Elastics vary greatly in quality and texture. The most successful are those that are smooth and very firm, as softer elastic is usually distorted by the stitching. The construction of the elastic can also distort the patterns, so it is important to work some small samples first. Some heavily ribbed elastic can create an interesting 'stepped' effect when stitched with satin stitch.

Because the embroidery must retain a high degree of elasticity, it is necessary to work lengthwise down the strip, choosing a stitch pattern that can be expanded without breaking. A fairly open satin stitch, and patterns based on this, are effective and successful.

Embroidered elastic is inexpensive and makes wonderful accents on children's clothes and sportswear.

MATERIALS

Firm woven elastic, at least
*   25 mm (1 in.) in width*
Machine threads in bright colours, plus
*   bobbin thread to match elastic*
Machine needle, size 90
Satin-stitch foot

METHOD

1 Thread the machine with the first bright colour, and the bobbin with a colour to match the elastic. Set the stitch length to fairly close, about 0.8 for an open satin stitch, and the stitch width at zero, to begin. Don't sew a very close, dense satin stitch as this creates waves in the elastic. Bring the bobbin thread up through the elastic and anchor the thread. Begin sewing with satin stitch, increasing and decreasing the stitch width as you sew, and moving in smooth, tapered curves from side to side on the elastic. Do not sew within 2–3 mm ($^1/8$ in.) of the edge, as this may distort the elastic.

2 With the second colour threaded through the needle, sew another row of tapering satin stitch, crossing over the first row, then sewing a wide stitch over the narrow section of the first row, and vice versa. Stitching in this way helps to prevent a heavy stitch build-up, which distorts the elastic.

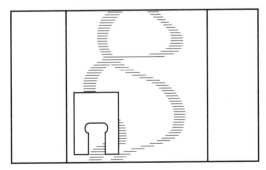

Finish with a few short straight stitches to secure the thread.

3 For 25 mm (1 in.) width elastic, two to three rows of stitching will be sufficient. For 150 mm (6 in.) wide belt elastic, several more rows may be added. In the belt shown in the picture on page 26, four rows of different colours were sewn first, and then shorter lines of accent colours were added.

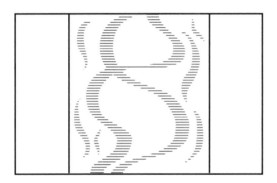

4 For the small coloured shapes within the lines, one unit of an automatic pattern has been used, with the machine programmed to stop after each unit. To do this manually, sew a very short length (5 mm or 1/4 in.) of satin stitch tapering to stitch width zero at each end of the shape.

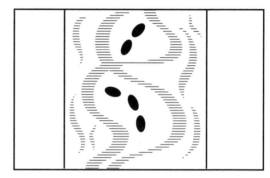

5 When the embroidery is completed, stretch the elastic to its required length to check for any broken stitches. Restitch if necessary.

BACKWARDS AND FORWARDS

SEWING WITH UTILITY STITCHES AND REVERSE

When I do a demonstration for a group of high school students, one of the first techniques I show them is this method of 'drawing' with the machine using the reverse button. Creating patterns and pictures in this way, with the feed teeth operating, is less frightening for beginners than working with free embroidery and the darning foot. It also helps to develop coordination and provides good practice in sewing quickly, both valuable skills for more complex techniques.

My new students are often asked to do an aptitude test for machine embroidery. They then discover that this involves patting their heads, rubbing their stomachs, stamping one of their feet and whistling simultaneously. The class usually dissolves into laughter, while I make my point that this silly exercise has much in common with embroidery skills, where I'm using the foot pedal, guiding the fabric with one hand and changing the stitch width or using the reverse button with the other. All done at speed, and possibly while discussing homework or chatting with the family. As several students have told me, anybody coping with the many demands of a spouse and kids is usually an expert at doing lots of things at once!

This forwards and reverse technique is useful for discovering how to say 'more with less'. Even if your machine only does a few very basic utility stitches, it is worth experimenting to find how many intricate and complex textures you can create just by working backwards and forwards, and moving your fabric as you sew. Some machines will not sew backwards in a pattern stitch, so check your instruction manual first. To use this technique on garment fabrics where stiff interfacing is not desirable, fabric may be firmly stretched in an embroidery hoop.

MATERIALS

Very firm even-weave fabric, stiffened with heavy iron-on interfacing
Machine thread in contrasting colour
Machine needle, size 80 or size 90
Zigzag foot

METHOD

1 Thread the machine top and bobbin with standard sewing thread in a colour to contrast with the background fabric. Attach the zigzag foot, and set the stitch length to medium and the width to zero. Place the fabric under the foot, bring the bobbin thread to the top of the fabric and anchor the thread. Cut off the ends. Experiment on some scrap fabric first. Run the machine fast, and sew all over the fabric, moving the fabric as you sew, so the stitching forms wavy lines, spirals and circles. *Do not pull the fabric against the direction of the feed teeth. Allow the teeth to pull the fabric, just use a very light touch of your left hand to guide it.*

2 Next, sew forward in a straight line, then without changing speed, press and hold the reverse button, allowing the machine to sew backwards. Practise this several times, guiding the fabric with your left hand and operating the reverse button with your right. It is important to keep the machine running at full speed. The grass stems in the picture were stitched in this way.

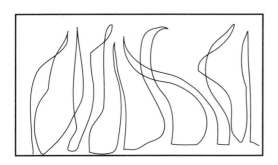

3 Change to a serpentine or three-step zigzag stitch. Keep the length at medium, but reduce the stitch width to 1.5 or 2. Move in short lines of 2–3 cm ($3/4$–$1^1/4$ in.), moving forwards and

backwards in a radiating pattern. This forms the seed heads on the grass stems.

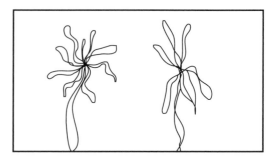

4 Change to a blind hemming stitch (several straight stitches followed by one zigzag). To form the spiky leaves, stitch up one side, tapering the stitch width to a point at the top, then stop and turn, and sew down the other side, increasing the stitch width to maximum back at the bottom. A different effect can be achieved by turning to the other side at the top, so the 'spikes' are pointing towards the centre of the leaf.

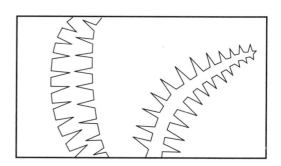

5 Experiment also with tight clockwise and anticlockwise spirals with blind hemming stitch, which can give interesting prickly seed heads or petalled shapes.

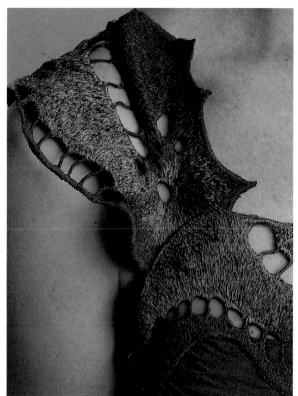

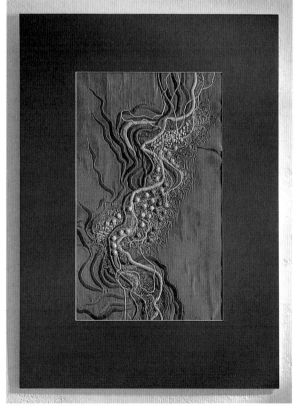

Above and top right: *Blue butterfly wing cutwork yoke* (page 106)

Right: *'Low Tide on the Reef'* (page 88)

Above: *Embroidered denim pencil case* (page 34)

Above and top left: *Samples of embroidered printed fabric* (page 48)

6 The sample shown in the picture on page 96 creates a simple picture of grass seed heads, but exciting abstract effects can be created using bright colours on dark fabrics. Remember, for softer garment fabric, stretch the background fabric in a hoop.

RAFFIA HAT WITH RIBBON LACE FLOWERS

My friend, Mardi, was stitching away industriously during a hot afternoon at the Mac-Gregor Summer School in Toowoomba, Queensland. By the end of the day, Mardi had transformed a very weatherbeaten old gardening hat into a floral creation the Queen Mother would have adored.

Mardi's method uses yarn, ribbon or raffia, couched onto soluble fabric; each hoopful of couching makes one flower. These are also effective with woollen yarns as lacy additions to handknitted garments.

The modular method, making small motifs and then arranging them, is a good one for beginners, as many different small samples can be grouped together for greater effect.

The flowers used in the picture on page 25 are made from a dyed nylon ribbon, but any firm ribbon or yarn would be equally successful. Several colours can be combined within one flower to give a subtle shading.

MATERIALS

Raffia hat
Ribbon, raffia or plastic gift tie ribbon, approx. 5 mm (^{1}/$_5$ in.) wide (allow 5 metres (5^1/$_2$ yards) per flower)
Cold- or hot-water soluble fabric (allow one 25 cm (10 in.) square for each flower)
Spring-loaded embroidery hoop, 20 cm (8 in.) size
Machine thread to match ribbon
Couching foot
Machine needle, size 90
Fabric glue or glue gun
Additional dried flowers, if desired

METHOD

1. The soluble fabric may be used as one large piece, with many flowers embroidered on it, or you may prefer to use small squares, each just large enough for the hoop, or leftover scraps of soluble fabric, overlapping them in the hoop if they are not large enough. Stretch the fabric in the hoop, rolling up any excess and securing it with spring clips. Set the stitch length to a medium straight stitch for a 5 mm (^{1}/$_4$ in.) wide ribbon. For raffia or plastic ribbon that may split, use a serpentine stitch, length about 1.5 and just wide enough to cover the ribbon. This stitch helps to keep the ribbon flat — a zigzag stitch tends to roll it into a cord.

2. Place the hoop under the needle and attach the couching foot. Bring the bobbin thread up through the

fabric and anchor the threads. Clip off the thread ends. Thread the ribbon or raffia through the front of the foot and lower the presser foot lever. Sew around the hoop in small, overlapping circles, making sure that each loop of ribbon is connected, or you will have a hole when the backing is dissolved. Make sure you sew several times over the cut ends of the ribbon so that it will not unravel.

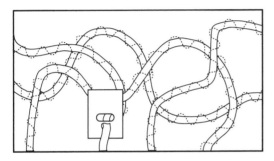

3 For a contrast, sew a second colour over the first, moving around in a figure-of-eight design as shown below.

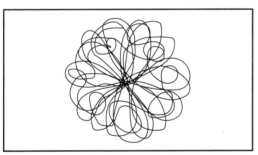

4 The hat in the picture (see page 25) uses ten flowers, each about a 15 cm (6 in.) circle when dried.

Dissolve the backing fabric in hot or cold water. Place the lacy circles on a towel to dry or iron dry, using a pressing cloth.

5 Twist the centre of each circle into a point, to gather it up into a flower shape. Secure with a short length of matching ribbon.

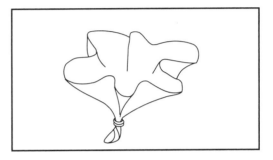

6 Arrange the lace flowers evenly around the band of the hat, holding each one in place with a pin. Secure with a little hot glue or fabric glue, removing the pins as the glue dries.

7 Arrange additional dried flowers in the spaces between the lace flowers, if desired, gluing in place.

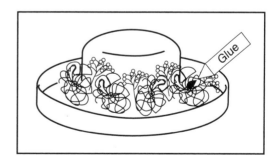

47

EMBROIDERING PRINTED FABRIC

This technique should really have been entitled 'Short Cuts and Cheating'. Even though the nuns at boarding school spent quite a lot of time encouraging me to improve my hand embroidery, not even the missions wanted what I had spent my Saturday afternoons unpicking, bleeding into and crying over. I wish I'd known then how much agony I could have avoided by using the machine instead.

This project is definitely a 'cheat'. The resultant machine-embroidered fabric is firm and rich in colour and texture. Embroidering printed fabric is suitable for small accessories, purses, spectacle cases, picture frames, etc. If you are more ambitious, a larger piece would look wonderful on an antique chair or foot stool. Dressmaking thread gives a stronger, more matt finish for articles that will be handled or used often.

When selecting fabric for embroidering in this way, choose a firm, even-weave material with a pattern that can be followed easily, preferably right across the fabric. Very irregular or wavy lines may be more easily stitched using the darning foot. Some of the automatic stitches on your machine may perfectly complement the printed pattern. Half the fun is experimenting. You may choose colours to either match or contrast with the print. The clever method of stitching the purse and attaching the lining gives a fast, very neat finish with no exposed seams, and only one line of final stitching.

MATERIALS

Cotton fabric or furnishing fabric
*   printed with suitable pattern*
Heavy iron-on interfacing
Taffeta for lining fabric
Button and silky cord or press stud for
*   bag closure*
Machine thread or machine
*   embroidery thread*
Satin-stitch foot, zigzag foot or
*   darning foot*
Machine needle, size 90, Metafil

METHOD

1 For the purse shown in the picture, cut a piece of printed fabric 25 cm x 40 cm (10 in. x 16 in.). It is important to make the background fabric stiff enough to take intensive embroidery without puckering, so cut two pieces of heavy, iron-on interfacing to the same size, and iron both onto the wrong side of the printed fabric. Thread the needle with a colour similar to one

of those in the printed fabric, and put a toning colour in the bobbin. Attach the satin-stitch foot. Loosen the top tension until the bobbin thread no longer shows and the silky thread does not break.

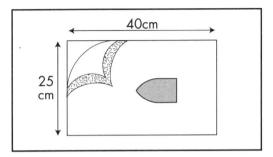

2 Practise on a sample of scrap fabric first. The samples shown on page 44 were sewn with:

(a) rows of satin and straight stitch (tartan)

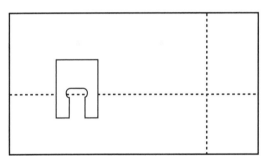

(b) an automatic pattern stitch (green and pink bargello)

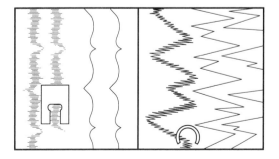

(c) medium width close zigzag, using the darning foot (blue zigzags).

3 In the samples shown, the pattern stitch only partially covers the background fabric, allowing the fabric colour to show through. You may choose your thread colour to match the background fabric exactly, or you may prefer a more subtle shading of colour. Using both matt and shiny threads gives a variety of highlights, and metallic threads can add a wonderful richness. You may also wish to use two threads together through the eye of a single needle. This works best when the machine is threaded as shown below (similar to the threading of a twin needle). The left-hand spool unwinds to the left and is threaded through the left-hand side of the tension disc, and the right-hand spool unwinds from the right and is threaded through the right-hand side of the tension disc.

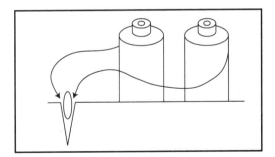

4 When the embroidery is completed, steam press the piece from the wrong side. Straighten and trim the edges. Cut a piece of lining to the same size as the embroidered fabric. Fold a 1 cm (1/2 in.) hem along the top edge to the wrong side of the fabric. Make another fold 14 cm (5½ in.) down from this folded edge, folding with the right sides together as shown. Press folds. Fold and press the piece of lining fabric exactly the same way. Now place embroidery and lining together — right sides together, wrong sides out — taking care to match folded edges exactly. Pin, then stitch a narrow seam around the three raw edges using a straight stitch. Shorten the stitch length to 1 as you sew around the corners.

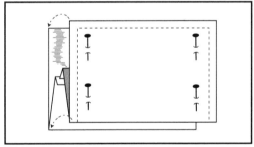

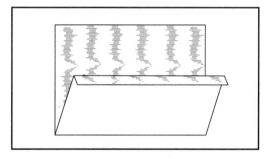

5 Trim seams and corners. Turn purse right sides out, pushing corners into shape. Press using a pressing cloth. Pin the open edge together and stitch close to the edge (use your blind hemming foot, and adjust your needle position to sew very close to the edge), or fuse the gap closed.

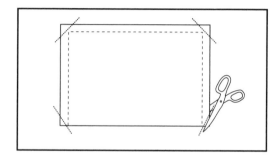

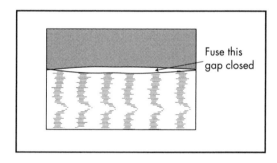

Fuse this gap closed

6 Attach a decorative button and loop, or press stud, to the front flap.

CUSHION COVER – SIMULATED SMOCKING

Anyone who has ever seen a sewing machine sales demonstration will remember how the salesperson effortlessly sewed lots of wonderful patterns, which were probably stitched on a folded piece of firm fabric that didn't pucker with all that pattern stitching. However, when the new machine came home and you sat down to sew rows of butterflies on a tablecloth, it didn't look nearly as good. This is because most machine embroidery is done successfully on fabric that is either stiff (such as cotton buckram, denim etc.) or stretched in an embroidery hoop. Chemical stiffeners (which give a paper-like stiffness to the fabric until washed out after embroidery) or stabilisers (stiff fabric or paper placed under the embroidery and torn away afterwards) are also often used to support the background fabric.

Yet sometimes mistakes can be turned to good advantage. This cushion cover shows a type of controlled puckering, where the wide satin stitch gathers up the fabric in regular patterns, creating an interesting textured surface, like a kind of false smocking. This technique can be used to create textured fabric to use for garments, accessories or artwork.

You may use a regular patterned fabric, like the Swiss cotton in the picture on page 95, or mark regular dots on the fabric with a fabric marking pen. You may prefer to work freely, gathering up the fabric in random areas. The thread may match or contrast with the fabric and, if your machine can be programmed to sew one unit of a pattern followed by several straight stitches, you may use this to create your own individual textures.

The most successful fabric to use is one that is soft and fine; one that gathers in easily. The completed fabric may be ironed to give a flatter, more creased pattern, or left soft and puffy for maximum contrast. Allow extra fabric for this technique, as the gathering effect will contract the material. Sew the false smocking first and then cut out the pattern piece required.

MATERIALS

Soft fine fabric, e.g. lawn, silk, Swiss cotton, batiste, plain or self-printed in a regular pattern
Matching or contrasting colours in machine thread
Open satin-stitch foot
Fabric marking pen

METHOD

1 To create a regular pattern, use a self-patterned fabric with small spots or lines spaced about 2–4 cm ($^3/_4$–$1^1/_2$ in.) apart, or mark a grid on the fabric with a marking pen. The fabric used for the cushion on page 95 is Swiss cotton, with small spots 3 cm ($1^1/_4$ in.) apart horizontally, and 2 cm ($^3/_4$ in.) apart vertically.

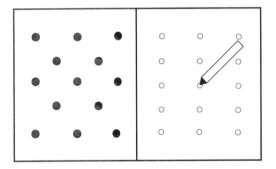

2 Thread the machine with the same colour on top and in the bobbin, using standard dressmaking thread — this is strong enough to hold the gathers together for washing by hand or machine. Attach the open satin-stitch foot (to allow the fabric to gather easily) and set the top tension to normal.

3 Make some small samples first to determine the pattern you like, and also to see how much your chosen pattern will contract the fabric. Several wide zigzags, with a stitch length that is very close, will pull the fabric together, as the open satin-stitch foot does not hold the fabric flat. (This effect, called tunnelling, is what you try to avoid with normal satin stitch, which should stay

flat.) Some individual units of pattern stitches, based on zigzag, may also have a similar gathering effect. The spacing between the gathered units and the directions of the rows will determine the pattern. Following are some of the variations you can try:

(a) ten very close zigzags (stitch length almost zero), followed by straight stitch to the next marked spot

(b) 1 cm ($^1/_2$ in.) block of wide satin stitch, followed by 2 cm ($^3/_4$ in.) of straight stitch

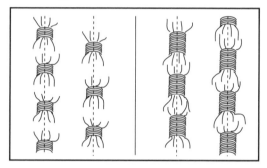

(c) 2 cm ($^3/_4$ in.) of satin stitch followed by 2 cm ($^3/_4$ in.) of straight stitch, with rows going horizontally and vertically

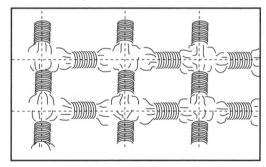

(d) single pattern units, e.g. a flower or satin stitch triangle, with straight stitch in between

(e) pattern stitch based on a circle, spaced with curving straight stitch between.

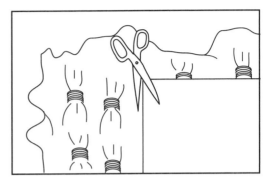

4 Make a note of the change in width and length of the fabric before and after the pattern stitching, so you can allow sufficient fabric to cut out your pattern pieces.

5 Do not iron the completed fabric if you like a very puffy effect. However, the fabric in the cushion shown was gently ironed from the wrong side before cutting and sewing up.

BANGLES
AUTOMATIC PATTERNS AND FABRIC PAINT

Many of the early books on machine embroidery devoted a great deal of space to instructions for matching patterns. This can be quite tricky, and I'm sure many of you have found, as I did, that a mismatched pattern (which usually occurs in a conspicuous area) can be both frustrating and disheartening.

This method of decorating fabric is fun and easy to do, and the closeness of the patterns, combined with dots of fabric paint, produces a richly coloured and textured fabric. It's also a good way of becoming familiar with all the pattern stitches on your machine, some of which may have never been used. If your machine only does basic utility stitches, experiment with these using lots of different bright colours. This project (shown on page 62) is an ideal way to use up short lengths of thread. As a rough guide, 1 metre (1 yard) of standard dressmaking thread will sew 4 cm (1½ in.) of 5 mm (¼ in.) wide satin stitch.

MATERIALS

Plastic bangle frame (available from craft stores)
Cotton fabric, preferably with fine stripes
Machine threads and embroidery threads
Machine needle, size 80, with large eye
Zigzag foot
Satin-stitch foot
Fabric glue
Glitter fabric paint
Liquid fabric stiffener or spray starch
Fabric marking pen

METHOD

1 Separate the inner ring from the bangle frame. Measure around the bangle frame and allow an extra 1 cm (½ in.) for a seam. Measure the width of the bangle frame, and allow an extra 2 cm (¾ in.) for turning and gluing. Cut a piece of paper to this measurement to use as a pattern. Fold one end of the pattern over to form a triangle (as shown below), cut it off and attach to the opposite end with masking tape. Your seam line will now follow the stripes on the fabric, making an inconspicuous join. As a guide, my pattern measures 5 cm x 27 cm (2 in. x 10¾ in.)

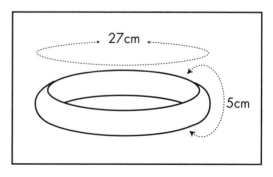

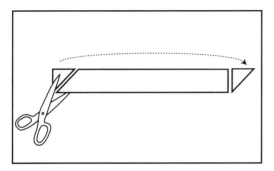

2 Trace around the pattern piece on the *bias* grain of the striped fabric as shown below, and cut a generous rectangle around it. Don't cut out just to the size of the pattern piece, as intensive embroidery may distort the fabric. Stiffen or spray starch the fabric until it is stiff enough to take pattern stitches without puckering.

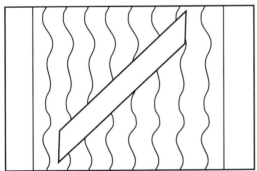

3 Thread the machine with your chosen colour, and use a colour to match the fabric in the bobbin. Select the correct foot for your pattern stitch: zigzag foot for patterns based on running stitch; and satin-stitch foot for wide satin stitch patterns. Loosen the top tension until the bobbin thread does not show.

4 Begin sewing 2–3 cm (^{3}/4–1^1/4 in.) outside the pattern line, using the stripes in the fabric as a guide, finishing 1–2 cm (^{1}/2–^{3}/4 in.) outside the pattern line. Sew several lines of one colour, changing stitches as required. Change thread colours and continue, alternating solid and lacy stitches, until the pattern area is completely covered with stitching.

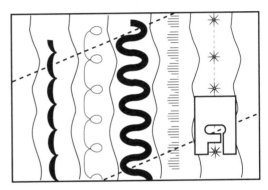

5 Rinse the fabric in cold water if necessary, to remove liquid fabric stiffener or starch. Dry, and iron the fabric from the wrong side. Replace the pattern piece on the right side, and retrace if necessary. Cut out the fabric along the traced lines.

6 Pin the embroidered piece around the bangle, wrong side out, stretching to ensure a snug fit. Pin,

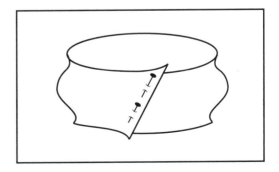

then stitch the seam using a short straight stitch. Trim seam to 3 mm (¹/₈ in.) and iron open.

7 Turn the fabric right side out and stretch it around the bangle, leaving an equal amount both sides for turning under. Run a line of fabric glue around the top inside edge of the bangle, allow a minute or two for the glue to become tacky, then carefully push the extra fabric to the inside. Repeat for the other side, pressing down firmly.

8 When the glue is dry, push the inner plastic circle into position, covering the raw edges of fabric. It should be a very snug fit. If not, secure with a little fabric glue.

9 Use the nozzle on the bottle of fabric paint to add fine dots to the embroidered patterns. Allow to dry.

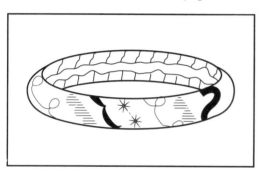

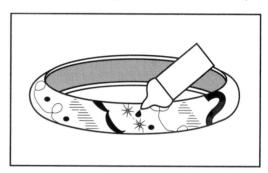

RIBBON LACE SHAWL

aking lace with soluble fabric is fun and fast. However, soluble fabric can become difficult to use during times of very high humidity, when everything feels damps and clammy. The only solution is to move into an air-conditioned environment, or wait for drier weather.

The colours shown in the picture on page 61 were made by dyeing rayon ribbon while still in the skein. However, any interesting exotic yarn or wool could be used instead. As a guide to quantities, the fringed shawl in the picture weighs 200 g (7 oz). Because the soluble backing is dissolved in very hot water, it is important that the yarn used is preshrunk. If you are not sure whether this is the case, make a sample of lace, trace the piece, wash and dry, and compare it with your tracing. If there is a noticeable difference, either preshrink the yarn or make your lace larger to allow for shrinkage.

The fringe can be applied with one or more yarns together, and used on clothing, cushions and accessories. A mixture of silky, mohair and velvet or chenille yarns looks thick and luxurious, and is also quick to make.

MATERIALS

*Knitted silky rayon ribbon,
   approx. 3–4 mm (1/8 in.) wide*
*Matching silky machine embroidery
   thread*
Hot-water soluble fabric
*Spring-loaded machine embroidery
   hoop, approx. 23 cm (9 in.) size*
White paint marker
Couching foot
Open satin-stitch foot
Machine needle, size 80, with large eye
Spring clips

METHOD

1 Tape the soluble fabric to the table, and use the white paint marker to trace the outline of the shawl. The one in the picture on page 61 measures 1.8 m x 0.6 m (2 yd x 3/4 yd) with a scalloped lower edge. Remember to leave at least 10 cm (4 in.) around the edge of the tracing, so the fabric can be stretched in the hoop.

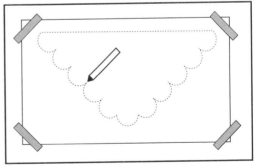

2 Beginning at one corner of the shawl, stretch the soluble fabric in the hoop. Roll up the excess fabric around the edge of the hoop and secure

with spring clips. Thread the machine top and bobbin with silky machine embroidery thread to match the ribbon and slightly loosen the top tension. Place the hoop under the needle, and attach the couching foot. Set the stitch width to zero, and the stitch length to medium. (For narrower ribbon or yarn, use a zigzag stitch just wide enough to cover the yarn.)

3 Bring the bobbin thread up through the soluble fabric, and make a few small stitches to secure. Cut off the thread ends. Feed the ribbon through the hole in the couching foot, and hold at the back of the work. Begin sewing down the ribbon, moving the hoop in curving lines so that the ribbon connects and overlaps. Sew until the ribbon covers the fabric, forming shapes approximately 1–1.5 cm ($^1/_2$–$^3/_4$ in.) across. Make sure all lines of ribbon are connected, or you will have a hole when the backing fabric is dissolved.

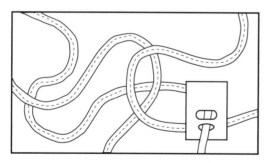

4 Finish sewing at one edge of the hoop. Without removing the hoop from the machine, release the inner hoop, and reposition on the next area to be stitched. Continue applying

the ribbon, sewing in smooth, flowing curves, and moving the hoop until the entire area inside the tracing is covered. Cover the raw end of the ribbon with some close forward and reverse stitching.

5 Remove the fabric from the hoop, and check by holding it up to the light. If any areas seem sparse or the ribbon is unattached, rethread the ribbon and continue stitching.

6 Trim any excess soluble fabric away from the edge of the shawl. To make the fringe, attach the open satin-stitch foot. (This is the easiest foot to use, otherwise use a satin-stitch or zigzag foot.) Set the stitch length to about 1.5 to 2 (slightly shorter than normal). Beginning at one corner, hold the end of the ribbon under the foot, and sew a few straight stitches to attach it to the edge of the lace, which is held to the right of the needle.

7 Lower the needle into the fabric, and raise the presser foot. With your left hand, hold the ribbon to the left, the required width of the fringe. (Mark the width required with masking tape on the machine extension table.) With the right hand, hold the other end

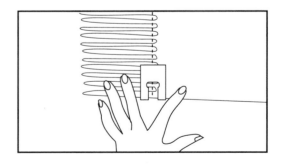

of the ribbon to the right under the needle. Hold the yarn down on both sides of the needle with the spread fingers of the left hand, and lower the presser foot. (This is much simpler if you have a presser-foot knee lift.) Stitch until you are one stitch past the end of the ribbon, and stop with the needle down.

8 To make the next loop, raise the presser foot lever, and wrap the yarn around the needle, across to the width marked on the machine table, and then back under the foot again. Lower the presser foot, and continue with a few more stitches. Keep the yarn ball in a box or basin on your right. This all sounds as if you need three hands, and although the method is certainly simpler using a knee-lifted presser foot and a needle that automatically stops in the down position, it is not difficult to get into the rhythm and create fringe quite quickly. For a thicker, more luxuriant fringe, use several strands or strands of different yarns together. As you sew, make sure that all the fringe loops are attached to the lace, not just the soluble fabric.

9 At the end of the fringe, cut and fold the yarn end back on itself, and stitch several forward and reverse stitches to cover the raw end.

10 Sew another two rows of straight stitch close to the first row along the full length of the fringe to make sure all loops are firmly attached.

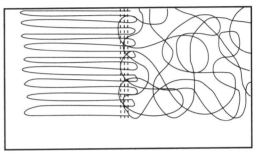

11 To remove the soluble fabric, rinse the shawl several times in very hot, soapy water until no trace of stickiness remains. Rinse well in cold water, and add a little fabric softener to the final rinse.

12 Peg the long straight edge of the lace to a clothes line in the shade to dry. For very delicate yarns, you may prefer to stretch and pin the lace to shape on a sheet spread over the carpet. If necessary, when dry, press with a warm iron and a pressing cloth.

DANDELIONS

SEWING WITH INDIVIDUAL PATTERN UNITS

The modern automatic embroidery machines lend themselves to many fascinating variations. Although early machine embroidery books concentrated on extremely precise matching patterns, usually symmetrical, I find it much more interesting to see what can be achieved by taking the pattern, or an individual pattern unit, as a starting point and developing a much freer design. This particular exercise was developed to encourage students to use the presser-foot knee lift available on many Bernina machines. The result has proved so popular that I have included instructions for both automatic and manual machines, with and without a knee lift.

The single-pattern-unit button is available on many of the latest machines. If your machine does not have this feature, you can sew a little more slowly, watching the progress of the pattern, and stop when each unit is completed. If you have a very simple machine that does only the most basic utility stitches, it is possible to achieve some interesting results with similar effect by using small blocks of satin stitch instead.

If you plan to use this technique on a garment, be careful not to make the connecting threads between the patterns too long, as they may catch and pull while being worn. The picture shows a circular design (see page 96), but linear designs, running over ribbons or along a border, are also possible.

MATERIALS

Backing fabric supported by iron-on interfacing or stretched in an embroidery hoop
Machine embroidery thread, in three shades of one colour
Toning standard thread for the bobbin
Open satin-stitch foot
Zigzag foot
Machine needle, size 80, with large eye
Fabric marking pen

METHOD

1 Most machine embroidery is best done on either stiff or stretched fabric, which remains flat and is not distorted by stitching. Pictures are most easily done on a firm backing, but garments need to retain the fabric softness, so are best stitched with the embroidered area stretched in a wooden hoop. Mark the position of each dandelion with the fabric marking pen; if a hoop is being used, place it over a marked area.

Above: *Ribbon lace shawl* (page 57)

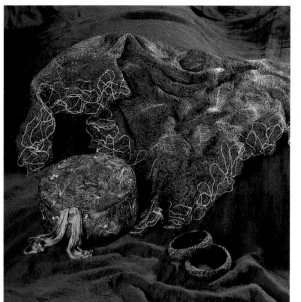

Above: *Blue lace scarf* (page 85), *minced fabric cocktail hat* (page 100) *and bangles* (page 54)

Above: *Cobweb lace collar* (page 73)

2 Thread the machine with the darkest shade to be used. Put a toning standard thread in the bobbin and loosen the top tension slightly, so that the bobbin thread does not show and silky threads do not break. Attach the zigzag foot. Set the stitch width to zero, and the length to medium for a straight stitch. Bring the bobbin thread up through the fabric and anchor the threads. To make the stems, sew two rows of straight stitch, ending at the centre point of each dandelion. Finish each stem with a few very short straight stitches.

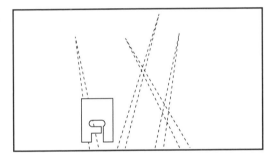

3 Attach the open satin-stitch foot. (This makes it easier to see the progress of each pattern.) Use the same colour as the stems. Choose a pattern stitch with small stars or circles. Select the single-pattern-unit button, if you have one. Make sure the threads are anchored. Begin by sewing one pattern unit in the centre of the dandelion, then stop, raise the presser foot and the needle, and move the fabric 2–3 cm (^{3}/4–1^1/4 in.) away to sew another pattern unit. It is important to raise the presser foot fully, as this releases the

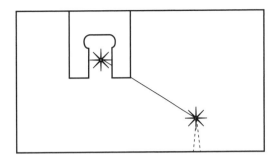

tension on the top thread so that it will not break when the fabric is moved. As you move the fabric, make sure that the connecting thread remains taut, or the machine will tangle the loose thread. Stop and move back to the centre of the dandelion, next to the first pattern. The connecting threads should lie very close to each other to form the delicate stalk of the floating seed.

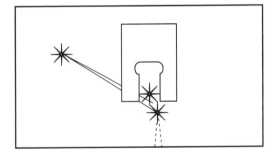

4 If you do not have a suitable automatic pattern, sew a small block (3 mm (^{1}/8 in.)) of a medium width satin stitch, beginning and ending on the right swing of the zigzag. Move the fabric straight to the right, and stitch another small block of satin stitch, beginning and ending on the left. Move the fabric to the left to sew the next block in the centre of the dandelion.

Beginning and ending in this way means that the connecting threads will come from the same side and lie close together.

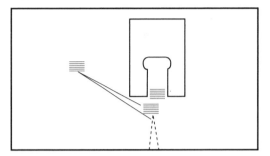

5 Using either step 3 or 4, continue in the same colour all round the dandelion, varying the length of each stalk slightly, and allowing the patterns in the centre to build up into a small circle approximately 15 mm (½ in.) in diameter.

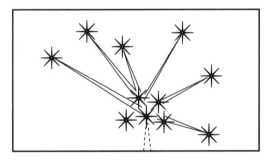

6 Change to a light colour and repeat, spacing the units in between those of the first round.

7 For the final round, change to the lightest coloured thread, and repeat step 3 or 4, finishing with several extra patterns in the centre to add a highlight or correct the shape. Finish each dandelion with a few small straight stitches to anchor the threads. Your final pattern will resemble one of the diagrams below.

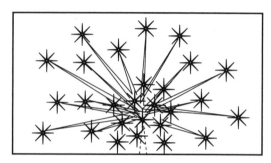

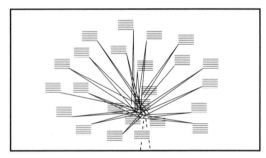

8 Work more dandelions in this manner, and also work some incomplete ones as shown in the picture on page 96. Try to avoid a stiff geometric form for a more natural look.

TWIN-NEEDLED VEST

About three years ago, I was asked to create an elegant fabric length in calico, to be made into a dinner jacket for a male friend to wear to an important fashion event.

First the calico was professionally stripped and dyed black — no easy feat, as all the stiffening and finishing must first be removed from the fabric. A length of fabric was then cut for each garment piece, allowing extra for the 'shrinkage' caused by all those twin-needled lines. Each piece was intensively stitched, in a random wavy line pattern, giving a very complex surface. Additional fabric was twin-needled, couched with black metallic cord, and re-embroidered with automatic pattern stitches, to make accent fabric for the shawl collar and turn-back cuffs of a gentleman's smoking jacket. The embroidered fabric was then sent to a dressmaker, who made up the garment.

When I later saw my friend wearing it, my heart sank. The pattern had apparently been made to suit a small, wide figure, and my friend is tall and slim. The moral of this story is: check your pattern shape and size first!

Twin-needled fabric can be used effectively on garments or accessories. This sampler vest (pictured on page 25), utilising many different twin-needled patterns, is a good exercise to begin with, allowing plenty of room for experimentation. Standard dressmaking thread is the most suitable for this technique, but keep in mind that some metallic and silky threads perform better when used in a special large-eye needle. Different colours can be used in each needle for added excitement.

When sewing automatic pattern stitches, it is important not to exceed the maximum stitch width your twin needle can safely sew. Many modern machines have an automatic twin-needle button that safely monitors the width of any pattern stitch chosen. *Never* stop and turn with the twin needle in the fabric. When continuously twin-needling a piece of fabric, it is much easier to fold the fabric into a tube, so you can continue to sew around and around without stopping to cut threads. If your fabric piece is not long enough, attach some extra 'junk' fabric to make a piece that will extend comfortably around the free arm of your machine. Remember to allow extra fabric as each twin-needled line will reduce the width very slightly. Twenty or thirty lines over a sleeve or bodice can reduce the width significantly. Choose simple garment patterns without complicated seams or darts.

MATERIALS

Even-weave cotton fabric for vest
Fabric for lining (e.g. lawn)
Vest pattern, without darts or tucks
Standard machine thread
Twin needle, 2 mm (¹/₈ in.) size
Pintuck foot or satin-stitch foot
Zigzag foot
Fabric marking pen
Fusible hem webbing

METHOD

1 Trace the basic vest pattern shapes onto an extra sheet of paper, remembering to make a separate piece for right front and left front, and draw vertical and horizontal lines to create the pieces to be rejoined later. Mark each piece carefully so that you will be able to reassemble them correctly. Also mark grain lines and add seam allowances. Cut out the paper pieces.

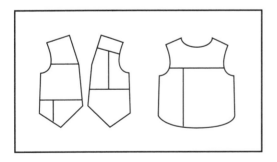

2 Place the paper pieces on the fabric, making sure grain lines are all going the same way. It is easier to twin needle larger pieces of fabric that can fit around the free arm of your machine for continuous sewing, so arrange your pattern pieces so that two or more may be cut from one piece of twin-needled fabric. Remember to allow extra fabric, as the stitching will cause the fabric to contract. Cut a rectangle of fabric for each group of fabric pieces to be stitched with the same pattern. Mark two or three grain lines on the full length of each fabric piece as a guide to use while sewing.

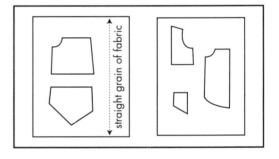

3 Attach the pintuck foot or satin-stitch foot. Thread the machine with standard dressmaking thread on top and in the bobbin. For the top threading, if possible, place the left spool with the thread coming from the left and passing through the tension disc on the left and through the left needle, and the right spool coming from the right and passing through the right-hand side of the tension disc and then to the right needle. This helps to reduce tangling and snagging. Tighten the bobbin tension slightly. This may be done on some machines by threading the bobbin thread through the finger on the bobbin, or by turning the small screw on the side of the bobbin in a clockwise direction. Consult your machine instruction manual if you are not sure.

4 To begin, place the fabric under the needle, close to one of the marked grain lines. Hold all three threads to the back of the work. Sew the first line while moving the fabric from side to side, to create a gently waving line. The twin-needle stitching will form a raised ridge.

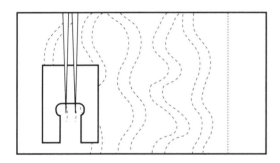

5 Stop sewing about 2 cm (³/4 in.) from the end of the fabric, and wrap the fabric around under the free arm (remove the sewing extension surface first!) and position the top end so it butts up against the bottom end, forming a tube, with long sides aligned.

6 Continue sewing across the join, so the second row of stitching is about 1–2 cm (¹/2–³/4 in.) away from the first. Keep moving around the fabric in this way, making lines in a random wavy pattern. If you prefer, you can space the lines more closely, or even allow them to cross here and there. Remember that each line will narrow the fabric slightly.

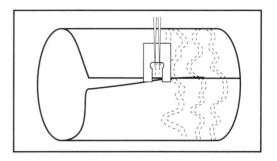

Keep an eye on the marked grain lines so that you don't sew too far off course. Remove the completed fabric from the machine, snip the connecting threads, and iron gently from the wrong side. Check the bobbin from time to time, as it is difficult to continue sewing neatly if the bobbin runs out in the middle of a row.

7 To complete the other pieces, try stitching in several different patterns. It is important to choose a narrower stitch width that does not allow the needle to hit the side of the foot; alternatively, engage the automatic twin-needle button. These are some suggested patterns: straight rows, spaced at one presser-foot width; straight rows at right angles, to form a square lattice pattern; straight or wavy rows using a

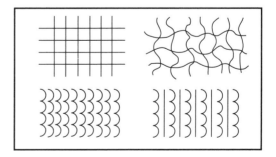

utility stitch, e.g. serpentine or three-step zigzag; matched or random scallops; alternating straight and patterned rows.

8 When all the pieces are completed, iron gently from the wrong side. Lay out all the paper pattern pieces on the embroidered fabric, arranging them so that adjacent pieces have different patterns. Remember to add seam allowances to these pieces if you have not already done so — this means the original main pieces will be the correct size when the patchwork is reassembled. Cut out the fabric and pin seams reassembling main pattern pieces.

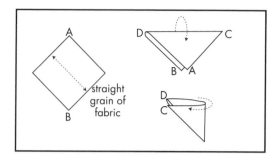

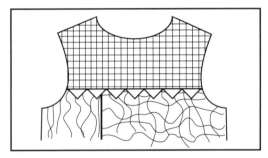

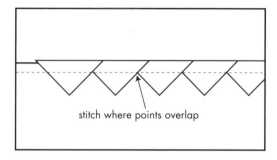

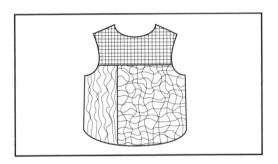

9 To make the triangular points inserted in some seams, fold and press several 6 cm (2½ in.) squares of fabric cut on the straight grain. Arrange the squares as shown — along one seam line and overlapping slightly, with open sides pointing in the same direction — and stitch. Pin the other pattern piece in position and sew just inside the first line of stitching. Trims seams and iron. Sew and iron open shoulder seams of vest.

10 Cut out the lining for the vest and sew the shoulder seams together. Iron the seams open. Place vest

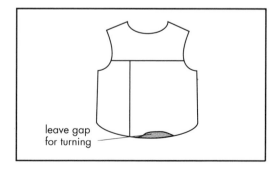

and lining right sides together and sew armhole, front and neck seams. Trim and iron. Sew side seams in one continuous line from lining to vest. Sew the bottom edge together, leaving a 15 cm (6 in.) opening at centre back for turning. Turn vest right side out and iron, neatening opening. Close opening with a small strip of fusible hem webbing.

11 Topstitch right around edges of vest and armholes.

BEDJACKET – QUILTED SCRAP PATCHES

When I was very young, I suffered dreadfully from bronchitis, aggravated by every bleak Melbourne winter. I can still remember how special I felt when tucked up warmly in bed, wearing Mother's best quilted pink satin bedjacket, with a fire crackling in the grate, watching the cold rain streaming down the windows.

Now I live in Sydney, and the bronchitis, thankfully, is a rare occurrence. The bedroom fire is a long-lost luxury, but I still have a couple of glamorous bedjackets, gifts from an adored mother-in-law with expensive and exquisite taste. For those days when the flu makes me miserable, it's a comforting remembrance of childhood to wear one while curled up in bed with pink tissues, soft music, a mushy romance novel and the fervent hope that one of my family is creating a minor culinary miracle in the kitchen.

The following technique is a fast and effective way to create a rich and warm fabric (see picture on page 26). Fine net covers a multitude of raw edges. The silky knitted braid quilts and decorates in one process. Glamorous evening wear is also possible, using metallic scraps and brocades. Some of the new chenille yarns would give a lovely velvety contrast to all that glitter. Choose a very simple pattern, preferably one with the sleeves and bodice in one piece, to eliminate bulky seams.

MATERIALS

Garment pattern
Sufficient soft lawn to line fabric
Lightweight woven iron-on interfacing
Lightweight quilt wadding
Fine net or tulle
Assortment of silky, sheer and light cotton scraps, cut into random pieces approx. 5–10 cm (2–4 in.)
Tubular silky knitting yarn, approx. 3–4 mm ($^1/_8$ in.) wide
Standard sewing machine thread
Zigzag foot
Walking or dual-feed foot, or cording foot with a large hole
Machine needle, size 80
Satin ribbon or button for fastening
Safety pins
Baking paper

METHOD

1 Preshrink lining, interfacing and knitting yarn. Arrange pattern pieces for the back and left and right front on the interfacing. Cut a rectangle around each one, leaving a generous 3–4

70

cm (1¹/₄–1¹/₂ in.) border to allow for contraction of the fabric during embroidery. Cut lining and quilt wadding to the same size as the interfacing for each piece.

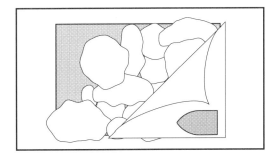

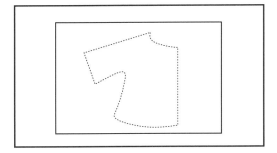

2 Place the iron-on interfacing on the table, glue-side up. Assemble your collection of scraps and begin placing them, overlapping very slightly, over the interfacing to form a random patchwork. You may wish to iron your fabrics flat first, or use slightly crumpled pieces to add textural interest. Don't use anything too crumpled, as it may be too thick for the needle to pass through. Use scraps of sheer fabrics over the top to cover any interfacing still showing, or blend edges of colours. Each scrap should be in contact with some of the iron-on interfacing so it will stick to the backing.

3 Cover the arrangement with some baking paper (to prevent fine or synthetic fabrics from melting) and iron with a fairly warm to hot iron until all the pieces are fused. If any small areas have not adhered, use the tip of the iron directly over the fabric until fused.

4 To make the quilt sandwich, place the lining fabric on a flat, smooth surface, wrong-side up, and tape the corners to the table with masking tape to keep everything smooth while you're pinning. Cover with a layer of lightweight quilt wadding and then the patchwork piece, right-side up. The top layer is fine net or tulle, to hold everything together and cover all the raw edges. Pin through all layers with safety pins, pinning every 10 cm (4 in.).

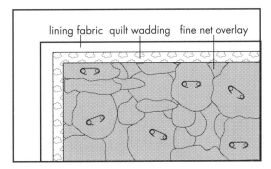

lining fabric quilt wadding fine net overlay

5 Thread the machine with standard sewing thread in a colour to match the yarn on top and to match the lining in the bobbin. Attach the walking or dual-feed foot. (If you don't have one, use the couching or braiding foot, and support the fabric from the underneath while sewing, watching for puckering.) Select a serpentine stitch, length and width about 2.5.

6 Beginning at one edge of the quilting, bring up the bobbin thread and anchor the threads. Thread the yarn through the needle slot in the base of the walking foot and hold the end behind the foot. Begin sewing across the fabric, supporting the quilted layers with one hand underneath, and moving in flowing lines, crossing and recrossing the fabric until you have created shapes approximately 3–4 cm (1¹/₄–1¹/₂ in.) in diameter. The 3–4 mm (¹/₈ in.) width of the yarn should flow smoothly through the foot and be fully

attached by the stitching. If you are using a narrower yarn, hold it with your right hand so that it feeds straight into the foot, rather than at an angle, which may allow the yarn to be missed by the stitching. Finish sewing at the edge of the fabric.

7 When all three pieces have been quilted, arrange the pattern pieces on top and cut out, making sure to cut a left and a right front. Complete garment to pattern directions, keeping seams narrow and neat (overlocking works well). Add lace frills at the sleeves, and a ribbon bow or button and loop closure at the front.

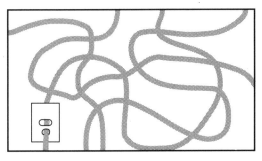

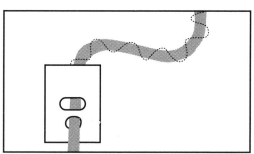

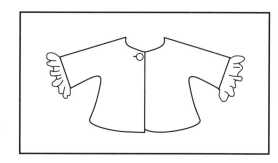

COBWEB LACE COLLAR

This delicate lace collar (pictured on page 62) is surprisingly easy to make, using a cotton knitting yarn couched onto soluble fabric. Most other forms of lacemaking use looped or plaited threads. However, this method uses a single strand, held together with fine spirals, making a delicate yet strong fabric.

It is important to make sure that the yarn you use is preshrunk, especially if you are using hot-water soluble fabric. If you are not sure, make a sample hoopful of the lace, dissolve the backing fabric, dry and compare the piece with the size of the hoop in which it was made. If there is any noticeable difference, you will need to preshrink the yarn. Place the skein of yarn (or wind the ball into a skein) in a tub of warm to hot water and soak for half an hour before draining and drying. This sample will also help you estimate the amount of yarn required. The completed collar may be handwashed after use.

MATERIALS
Water-soluble fabric
Paper pattern for collar
White paint marker
Spring-loaded machine embroidery hoop, 15–20 cm (6–8 in.) size
White cotton knitting yarn
White machine thread
Machine needle, size 80
Couching foot
Darning foot
Small pearl button
Piece of old calico or sheeting for pressing cloth
Small spring clips to secure rolled-up fabric

METHOD

1   Place the paper pattern flat on the table. If it is in two pieces, e.g. back and front, overlap the pieces at the seams and treat them as one pattern piece. As the collar is made in openwork lace, you will not need to worry about grain lines in the fabric. Place the soluble fabric over the pattern piece, leaving a generous allowance, e.g. 5 cm (2 in.), around the edge of the pattern so that the hoop can fit right up to the edges. Tape each corner of the soluble fabric to the table so that it will stay smooth as you trace.

2   Use the white paint marker to trace the outline of the collar onto the soluble fabric.

3   Remove the tape, and stretch the soluble fabric in the hoop, beginning at the neck edge of the centre

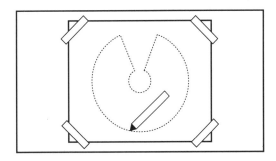

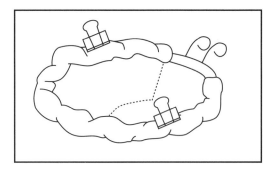

ball of yarn in a basin on the floor next to your chair or thread the ball onto the arm of your knee lift, if you have one. Lower the presser foot lever. Begin sewing, making sure that the zigzag stitch just covers the yarn. If it is too wide, the stitching will be loose when the fabric is dissolved. After a few centimetres of sewing, cut off the thread ends.

6 Use your left hand to steer the hoop and use your right hand to hold the yarn. Move across the hoop, making plenty of 'intersections' (several lines crossing at the same point), as these will be the centres of the 'spider web' spirals. Sew one line over the beginning of the yarn so that the raw end is covered. Make sure that all the lines connect, or they will not hold together when the background fabric is dissolved. When the area in the hoop is completely covered with connecting lines, making shapes no larger than 2–3 cm (^{3}/4–1^1/4 in.) and with 'intersections' spaced approximately 6–8 cm (2^1/2–3^1/4 in.) apart, finish stitching near the edge of the hoop.

back. Roll up the excess soluble fabric around the hoop, and secure with small spring clips. (Pins may tear the fabric.)

4 Thread the machine with white standard dressmaking thread top and bobbin. Place the hoop under the needle, and attach the couching or braiding foot. Set the stitch width just wide enough to cover the yarn with a zigzag stitch, and set the stitch length to medium. Check that the feed teeth are raised and the top tension is set to normal.

5 Bring the bobbin thread to the top of the fabric, and hold behind the foot. Thread the cotton knitting yarn through the hole in the couching foot, and hold the end behind the foot, with the thread ends. Place the

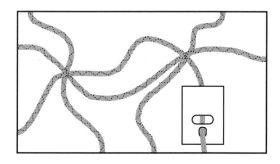

7 Raise the presser foot lever and release the inner spring hoop. Move the outer hoop (underneath the fabric) to the adjoining area and replace the spring hoop, making sure the fabric is taut. Roll up and clip any excess fabric. Lower the presser foot lever and continue sewing the yarn, making sure that you overlap smoothly onto the previously sewn area, so there are no gaps or obvious joins.

8 Continue in this way all around the collar shape, finishing at the neck edge of the centre back. You may wish to include a small loop of yarn to hold the button used for closing the collar. Cut the end of the yarn, and secure with a few forwards and reverse zigzag stitches to attach it invisibly. Change the stitch width to zero, and fasten off with a few straight stitches into the yarn.

9 Remove the couching foot and attach the darning foot. Lower or cover the feed teeth, and set the stitch length and width to zero. Run the machine fairly fast, and move the hoop slowly to create a small straight stitch. Sew down one of the lines of yarn to the centre of one of the 'intersections', then sew in a close spiral movement from the centre outwards until you have made a circle or web shape approximately 3–4 cm (1^1/$_4$–1^1/$_2$ in.) across. The lines of your spiral should be approximately 2–3 mm (^{1}/$_8$ in.) apart.

10 Sew down an adjacent line of yarn to the centre of another intersection and make another spiral. If the lines in your intersection are not evenly spaced, you may need to add an extra radial line of straight stitching to support the circle. Continue sewing spirals and moving the hoop as required until you have completed the collar.

11 Remove the hoop from the machine and release the fabric. Tack the collar to an old piece of calico or sheeting, using thread in a contrasting colour. This will help to support the delicate lace while the background is dissolved. Dissolve the backing fabric in hot or cold water. Rinse well until no trace of stickiness remains.

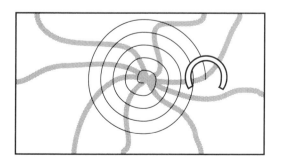

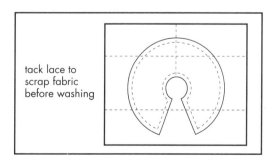

tack lace to scrap fabric before washing

12 Spread the collar, lace-side down, on a table covered by a thick bathtowel. Using the calico or sheeting as a pressing cloth, ease the collar into shape, with the iron on a medium setting. When the collar is thoroughly dry, remove the tacking threads. Attach a small pearl button for fastening, corresponding with the loop on the opposite side.

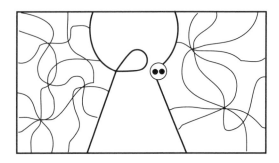

GOLD NECKLACE

Jewellery made on the sewing machine can be as exotic or precious as you want to make it. This rich-looking collar (pictured on page 26) is made from fabric scraps, gold embroidery threads and cords, and stitched onto hot-water soluble fabric. The little gold rings, which give the collar some weight, are small brass washers and rings donated by the handyman father of a friend who found them at a garage sale. Every stitch is done by machine, but take extra care when attaching metal rings or beads.

These same techniques can be adapted for making larger pieces, which could be attached to a backing for high-relief artwork, or mounted on a base or suspended for a three-dimensional piece. Other varieties of found objects — e.g. bones, shells, wood or wire — could be incorporated, with the lacy embroidery forming a flexible textured contrast.

MATERIALS

Gold metallic machine embroidery thread and matching silky thread for bobbin
Hot-water soluble fabric
Small scraps of metallic fabric
Scraps of paper-backed fusible webbing
Fine gold cord for couching
Small brass washers and rings, and a few gold beads

White paint marker
Spring-loaded machine embroidery hoop
Machine needle, size 90, Metafil
Couching foot
Darning foot
Small spring clips to secure rolled-up fabric

METHOD

1 The pattern for the necklace can be derived from an existing piece of jewellery, or made by cutting paper shapes and arranging and pinning them until you create a pleasing design. A collar or high-necked bodice can be used to give the required neck shaping.

2 Place the paper pattern on the table, and spread the hot-water soluble fabric on top, taping the corners to the table to keep the fabric flat as you trace your pattern with the white paint marker. Remove the tape. Place the paper-backed fusible webbing glue-side down on the wrong side of the pieces of

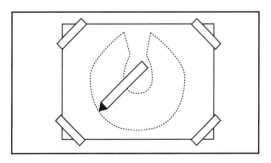

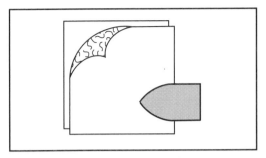

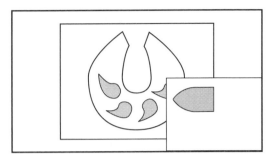

metallic fabric, and cover with a pressing cloth. Iron, being careful not to melt the fabric, until the glue has melted and fused.

3 Fold each piece of backed fabric in half, fabric side together, and pin. Draw your shape/s onto the paper side, and cut out. This will give you two mirror-image shapes. Peel the backing paper off one shape and arrange it in

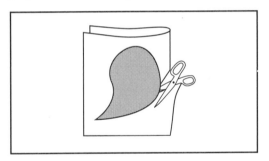

place, glue-side down, on the hot-water soluble fabric. Cover with a pressing cloth, and press with a dry iron until fused. (Steam may melt the soluble fabric.) Turn the fabric over, and fuse the other mirror-image shape exactly on the back of the first shape. This double-sided fusing prevents glue being left uncovered on the back of the collar, and also adds firmness to the finished piece. Repeat for all shapes.

4 To prepare the piece for sewing, place the outer ring of the embroidery hoop under the back corner of the collar, and press the inner ring firmly into place, making sure that the fabric is tightly stretched. Roll up any excess fabric and secure with small spring-loaded clips. (Pins may tear the fabric.)

5 Thread the machine with metallic gold thread on top, and a matching silky embroidery thread in the bobbin. (Metallic thread used in the bobbin feels very scratchy when worn next to the skin.) Attach the darning foot, and lower or cover the feed teeth. Set the stitch length and width to zero. Loosen the top tension by several degrees, so that the fine metallic thread does not break.

6 Bring the bobbin thread up through the fabric by turning the handwheel, and lower the presser foot. Hold the thread ends gently, and make a few small stitches to anchor the threads before cutting off the thread ends. Begin to sew, running the machine fairly fast and moving the hoop smoothly in small overlapping circles that cover the back-

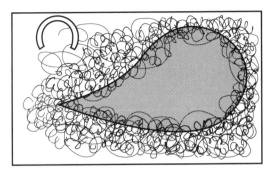

ground fabric fairly closely. When you come to an appliquéd piece of fabric, stitch in very small circles for 2–3 mm (1/8 in.) over the edges, to attach the fabric and prevent fraying (see diagram above).

7 When you have covered the area inside the hoop, look carefully to make sure there are no areas where the stitching is not connected, and finish at the side of the hoop closest to an unstitched area. Release the spring on the inner hoop and slide the outer hoop further along under a new area of fabric. Replace the inner hoop, making sure the fabric is tightly stretched. Continue sewing until you have covered the whole collar with a fairly dense pattern of small overlapping circles.

8 Remove the hoop from the machine, release the fabric and hold the collar up to the light to check for any thin or unattached spots. If necessary, replace the hoop and restitch. By now your collar should feel fairly firm and strong, so the next part of the project may be completed without stretching the fabric in an embroidery hoop.

9 Remove the darning foot, and raise or uncover the feed teeth. Set the stitch length to medium, and the width to a narrow zigzag, just wide enough to cover the fine metallic cord. Attach a couching foot with a fine hole or grooves. Place the fabric under the foot, beginning at the centre back. Thread the cord through the hole or groove at the front of the foot, and hold the cord and thread ends to the back of the work. Lower the presser foot and sew the cord to the collar, moving in large circles or curved lines. If you have a multigroove couching foot, you may wish to attach several cords at once, selecting a wide, close serpentine stitch.

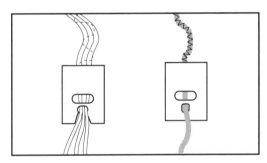

Stitch over the collar, finishing at the centre back with a small loop for fastening. Cover the cut ends of the cord with a little close zigzag stitching. Finish with a few short straight stitches. Attach a small gold bead or button to the corresponding place on the other side of the collar.

10 Gold beads may be added to the bottom of the collar for a fringed effect. Thread several beads onto a length of gold cord. Make a loop of cord about 2–3 cm (³/4–1¹/4 in.) long, with one or more beads hanging at the bottom of the loop. Use the open satin-stitch foot to sew a narrow zigzag down and up 2–3 mm (¹/8 in.) at the end of the loop to attach it to the collar, leaving the longest part of the loop hanging free. Repeat for each loop.

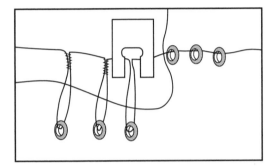

11 To attach the gold washers and rings, attach the darning foot, and lower or cover the feed teeth. Set the stitch length to zero, and the stitch width wide enough to clear the sides of the ring. Place the washer in position and lower the presser foot. Turn the handwheel for a few stitches to make sure that the needle clears the washer. Zigzag over the edge for about 20 stitches, then turn the stitch width back to zero, finishing with the needle outside the washer. Move the fabric slightly so that the needle does not hit the metal, and straight stitch carefully to the next position. Repeat, ending with a few straight stitches. You may also wish to embroider some extra thread 'beads' for added texture by repeating the same process, without using a gold washer, but just with the zigzag stitch, which will build up a hard little pile of thread similar to a real bead.

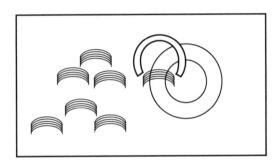

FLOWER SPRAY

A very good friend of mine, Evlyn, does the most beautiful floral work. One memorable weekend, she asked me to help her with the flowers for a very big wedding. The bride had requested an enormous bouquet to complement her copy of the royal wedding dress. I spent an hilarious Friday evening and Saturday morning sitting in Evlyn's father's cellar (the coolest spot during a Sydney heatwave) surrounded by racks and crates of bottles, and buckets and tubs of flowers. As the florist's 'junior', this was where I learned about wiring and taping flowers. Three hundred sticky, scented stephanotis flowers later, I had become quite proficient. After the ceremony, the 1.5 kg (3 lb), 90 cm (1 yard) long bouquet finished the weekend in the mother of the bride's bathtub.

The flowers you will make in this project (pictured on page 95) are a lot easier to work with, and will outlast the wedding to be displayed on a dressing table or mantelpiece. Smaller flowers can be incorporated into a corsage or hairpiece, or used to decorate a hat.

When choosing fabric for the flowers, test a small piece first by holding it over a candle flame. Nylon organza melts, making it easy to achieve a very neat finish along the cut edge, whereas silk and some synthetic fabrics burn or scorch. Be especially careful when working with light-coloured fabrics.

MATERIALS

Stiff, fine sheer synthetic fabric, e.g. nylon organza (20 cm (8 in.) is sufficient for 3 flowers or 8 buds)
Mylar threads or fine unravelled metallic threads
1 m (1 yd) ribbon for the bow
Machine embroidery thread to match fabric
Machine needle, size 80, Metafil
Zigzag foot
Paper-backed fusible webbing
Baking paper
Stiff florists' wire for stems
Fine florists' wire for wrapping round stamens
Green plastic florists' tape (Parafilm)
Plastic stamens (available from craft stores)
Candle, supported in a holder
Fabric marking pen

METHOD

1. Cut a strip of organza 20 cm (8 in.) wide and the width of the fabric (usually 115 cm (45 in.)). Cut in half vertically. Cut a piece of paper-backed fusible webbing the same size as one of the pieces. Cover your ironing

board with baking paper (so any glue melting through the fabric will not stick to the ironing board), and place one piece of organza on top. Cover with the paper-backed fusible webbing, *glue-side down.* Iron with a fairly warm iron until the glue is melted and fused to the organza. Remove the backing paper from the fusible webbing.

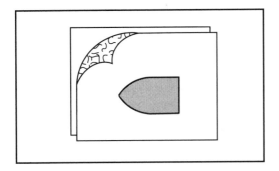

2 Tease out some mylar threads, or unravelled glitzy threads, and lay these over the glue, spreading them out so they form a fairly even layer. Cover with the second piece of organza, then another sheet of baking paper (so you don't get glue on the iron), and iron with a warm to hot iron until the two layers are fused together. Some synthetic sheers have a lower melting point, so

test a small area first before ironing the whole piece. The baking paper will also give some protection for fine fabric. Check that the glue is fused well, then remove baking paper. Fusing two layers together in this way stiffens the fabric, so you should not need any further stabiliser to support the fabric when sewing.

3 Cut a template from paper. The petal shape used in the picture on page 95 is approximately 10–12 cm (4–4½ in.) long, 5 cm (2 in.) wide and 3 cm (1¼ in.) wide at the base (so the petals can be gathered in slightly when wiring). Trace petal shapes along the fabric as shown below, slanting the shape so the length of the petal is on the bias grain of the fabric. (This helps the petals to curl slightly.)

4 Thread the machine with embroidery thread on top and in the bobbin, in a colour to tone with the fabric. Attach the zigzag foot. Set the stitch length and width to a close, very narrow zigzag. Don't use a satin stitch, as this tends to make the edges of the petals too thick. Loosen the top tension slightly. Sew around each petal. It's

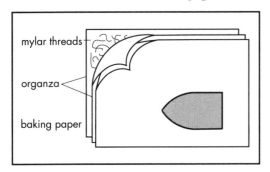

quicker to sew a short straight line from the end of one petal to the beginning of the next, rather than stopping and starting for each one.

5 Cut out each petal, using small sharp scissors and cutting close to the stitching. Stretch each petal gently to curl it slightly. Place the candle in a stable holder on a table. Make sure the room is free from draughts. Hold the petal about 10 cm (4 in.) above the flame, so that the heat melts and seals any raw edges outside the stitching. This is easier to see and control if the candle is at eye level, with the light coming from behind (e.g. in front of a closed window). Practise with a few spare or reject petals first.

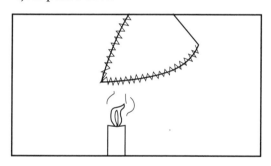

6 To make the flowers, first take five stamens and fold in half over a loop of fine wire. Twist wire twice to hold stamens firmly (a). Bend 1 cm ($\frac{1}{2}$ in.) of the end of the heavier stem wire as shown below (b), and attach the stamens to the bent end, with several twists of fine wire. Hold one petal next to the stamens, with the base extending past them and slightly gathered. Attach with a firm twist of fine wire, then

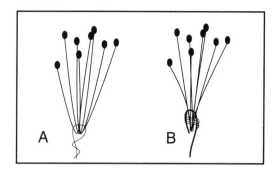

attach the next petal, slightly over-lapping the first. Continue until you have attached eight petals for the larger flowers, six for the smaller ones.

7 Cut a 30 cm (12 in.) length of plastic florists' tape. Stretch one end slightly (this makes it cling) and wrap firmly around the base of the petals, covering the wire. If you are right handed, first attach the tape to the base of the flower with a few wraps, then

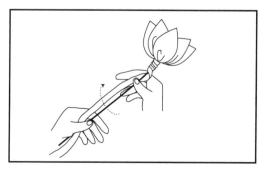

hold the tape in your left hand, stretching it slightly, about 5 cm (2 in.) from the flower. With your right hand, turn the flower stem and smooth the tape as it winds on, moving your fingers gradually down the stem. Resist the temptation to apply the tape like a bandage, as it will look thick and lumpy. Practise on a few stems of wire first.

8 To make the buds, cut a 15 cm (6 in.) square of organza on the straight grain. Fold the square diagonally twice, as shown below. Gather the open raw edge end of the triangle around the bent end of a stem wire, and secure with several firm twists of fine wire. Cover bud base and stem with florists' tape.

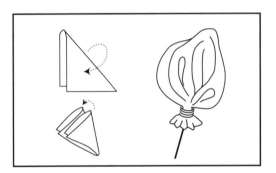

9 Assemble the spray, placing buds to the back and side, and arranging flowers so they overlap, and conceal stem wire. You may wish to include a few stems of natural dried flowers as well. Twist florists' tape around stems to hold them together. Trim wires to the desired length with wire cutters.

10 For a bridal bouquet, you may wrap the 'handle' of the spray with satin ribbon. Tie a large bow of ribbon or organza to finish the spray.

BLUE LACE SCARF

his work (pictured on page 62) was commissioned by Madeira Threads as an exhibition piece to display the versatility of their machine embroidery threads. It was a relaxing piece to make, as the repetitive movement of the hoop in small circles was quite hypnotic. I found myself moving to the rhythm of the background music, rather like an endless, leisurely Viennese waltz.

This is a simile I have often used with new students, who are sometimes a little tense and uncoordinated with their first efforts at free machine embroidery. 'Imagine you are waltzing or skating in the moonlight, with the "significant other" of your dreams,' I tell them.

This approach works well for those of us who remember the romance of ballroom dancing. The funky energetic beat preferred by teenagers is less successful, and more inclined to erratic movements!

For a silky finish in this piece, use machine embroidery thread; for a stronger, matt finish, use standard dressmaking thread.

MATERIALS

Machine threads in four colours (4 x 1000 m (1100 yd) spools for each colour)

Heavier silky cord or stranded embroidery thread for border
Machine needle, size 90, Metafil
Water-soluble fabric
Spring-loaded machine embroidery hoop, 23 cm (9 in.) size
White paint marker
Darning foot
Couching or braiding foot
Extra bobbins
Small spring clips to secure rolled-up fabric

METHOD

1 Tape the corners of the soluble fabric to the table to keep it smooth, and draw the outline of the scarf with the white paint marker. Leave at least 5 cm (2 in.) of fabric outside the pattern outline. Remove the tape and stretch the soluble fabric in the hoop, beginning at one corner. Roll up the excess fabric and secure with small spring clips.

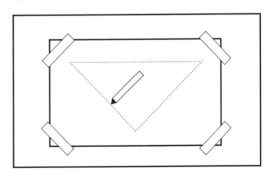

85

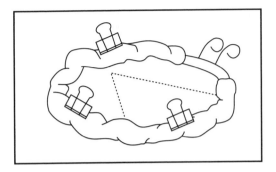

2 Thread the top of the machine with one colour and use a contrasting colour in the bobbin. It is convenient to have several bobbins wound in the different colours you will be using, so you can change top and bobbin threads often for a subtle shaded effect. Attach the darning foot, and lower or cover the feed teeth. Set the stitch length and width to zero. Loosen the top tension slightly. Place the hoop under the needle and bring the bobbin thread to the top of the fabric. Lower the presser foot lever, and hold the thread ends while you make a few small stitches, then cut off the thread ends. Run the machine fast, and move the hoop smoothly in small overlapping circles about 1 cm ($^1/_2$ in.) in diameter. Change top and bottom colours as required to achieve a subtle variation of colours.

3 When the area in the hoop is covered with stitching, check that there are no thin spots or unattached areas, and restitch any if necessary. Finish stitching at the edge of the hoop, and raise the presser foot lever. Release

the inner spring-loaded hoop, and slide the underneath hoop to an adjacent unstitched area. Replace the inner hoop, making sure that the fabric is taut. Roll up any excess fabric and secure with spring clips. Continue in this manner, filling in all areas inside the pattern. Check for any thin spots or unattached threads by holding the fabric up to the light. Restitch if necessary.

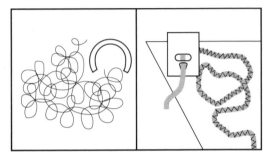

4 For the border, position the hoop over the area to be stitched. Raise or uncover the feed teeth, and set the stitch length to medium. Remove the darning foot, and attach the couching or braiding foot. Thread the accent cord through the braiding foot, and set the stitch width to a narrow zigzag, just wide enough to cover the cord. You may wish to use a top thread to match or contrast with the couched thread. Stitch in flowing lines round the edges of the scarf, moving the hoop as necessary. Finish the ends of the cord with some close stitching. Repeat for each accent cord.

5 Remove the fabric from the hoop, and wash carefully in hot or cold water to dissolve the backing.

Rinse well until no trace of stickiness remains. Place the lace on a flat, smooth surface into which you can push pins, e.g. a sheet spread over the carpet, and stretch and pin the lace gently into shape. Leave until completely dry. Repeat this stretching and pinning each time the lace is washed.

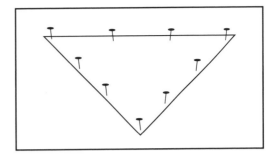

LOW TIDE ON THE REEF

RAISED STITCHING AND BARNACLES

In November 1993, I finished a month of travelling workshops around Queensland. The last stop was Cairns, where my husband joined me for a magical week of exploration of reefs and rainforests. As we flew home to Sydney on a brilliant afternoon, the reef we had been swimming over was spread beneath us — long, lazy curves of beige and ochre, shading into clear turquoise, aqua, mauve and blue. Even from several thousand feet, the reef was still one of the most beautiful things I have ever seen.

This picture (seen on page 43) is an attempt to capture a little of that magic, and also to suggest the rich texture and patterns of the coral at low tide. The raised bumps or 'barnacles' are an effective way of achieving a very defined surface.

A few words of warning for beginners: practise your barnacles on a piece of scrap fabric, and don't stop until you've done about six. The first three may be a bit shaky, but by the time you've done six, you should be much more successful. If you are using barnacles on garments, don't put them on hip pockets or anywhere you're likely to sit on them, as they are very hard.

Always make barnacles the very last technique you do on a piece of embroidery, as they are difficult to sew close to and impossible to sew over. If you are sewing barnacles onto a garment, stretch the fabric in an embroidery hoop.

MATERIALS

Firm backing fabric, e.g. cotton
buckram or two layers of very heavy
iron-on interfacing
Paper-backed fusible webbing
Shaded fabric for background,
e.g. painted silk or two layers
of organza
Machine embroidery threads in blues
and ochres
Firm fine and medium cord for
couching
Machine needle, size 90, with large eye
Satin-stitch foot
Darning foot
Couching foot
Fabric marking pen

METHOD

1 To make a firm backing fabric to support the embroidery, cut a piece of cotton buckram the required size. The one shown in the picture on

page 43 is 33 cm x 22 cm (13 in. x 8³/4 in.). Cut a piece of paper-backed fusible webbing and a piece of background fabric to the same size. Place the paper-backed fusible webbing *glue-side down* on the buckram and iron firmly with a hot iron until the glue is melted and fused. Peel off the paper. Place the background fabric, right-side up, over the glue and iron until the fabric is fused to the background. Check the heat of your iron first, so you don't melt synthetic or delicate fabric. If using iron-on interfacing, fuse two layers to the wrong side of the background fabric.

2 If you wish, outline the shapes you want to create in your picture onto your background fabric with a marking pen. I've used curving lines that flow from side to side. Thread the machine with a neutral colour in the bobbin, and select your first shade in blue embroidery thread for the needle. Attach the satin-stitch foot, and set the stitch width to maximum, and the stitch length to very close or 0.5. Bring the bobbin thread to the top of the fabric and anchor the threads. Cut off the thread ends.

3 The embroidery in this picture begins with the lowest, flattest stitches, and finishes with the most raised. This makes it easier to stitch, as you can sew over the flatter areas and leave the raised barnacles until last. Start by working several lines of satin stitch across the background, changing the stitch width gradually and moving the

fabric as you sew to form long, curving lines. Sew some shorter lines radiating out from one side. Repeat with several shades of blue and turquoise. To finish a line of satin stitch, gradually taper the stitch width to zero and end with a few short straight stitches. Clip the thread ends close to the fabric.

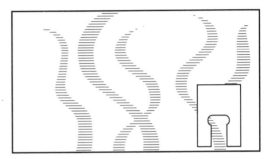

4 The lacy tracery of the dry coral reef is made by using a loose thread in the bobbin. Reduce the tension on your bobbin by turning the small screw on the side of a removable bobbin case gently to the left, as shown below, until the bobbin thread pulls freely and will not support the weight of the bobbin case when suspended. ('Right is tight; left is loose' is the way you remember which way to turn.) Always hold the bobbin case over a small box

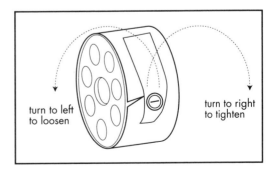

turn to left to loosen

turn to right to tighten

while turning the screw, as the screw is very tiny and impossible to find if you drop it. Make a note of how many turns you have made, so you can return the bobbin to the normal setting. It is easier to have a separate bobbin case set at the loose tension for this kind of work. If you have a drop-in bobbin, consult your machine's instruction book. Some machines get sulky if you play with your bobbin tension. If yours is one of these, do the next step with straight stitch, normal bobbin tension and a slightly loosened top tension.

5 Attach the darning foot and lower or cover the feed teeth. Set the stitch width and length to zero. Set the top tension to one or two points higher than normal. Use a standard thread on top, and matching embroidery or standard thread in the bobbin. Bring the bobbin thread up through the fabric, and lower the presser foot, holding the thread ends gently as you begin to sew. Run the machine fairly fast, and move the fabric *very* slowly, so the bobbin thread builds up in a raised line on the surface.

6 Move in either a cornelli movement or backwards and forwards in concentric lines as shown below. You may wish to use several shades of ochre as you sew, overlapping from the background and onto some of the satin stitch lines. Small tight close spirals give an interesting pattern.

7 Remember to return your bobbin tension to normal before moving on to the next step. For the raised lines of cording, attach the couching foot. Raise or uncover the feed teeth and set the machine to a narrow satin stitch, just wide enough to cover the fine cord you wish to use. Begin at one edge of the fabric, with the cord threaded through and under the foot, and all the thread ends held behind the foot. Sew gently

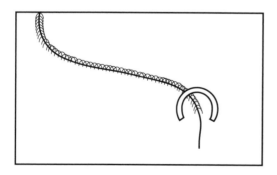

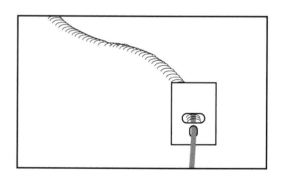

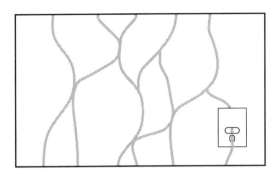

curving lines of cording up and down your reef. You may wish to sew over a previous line for a short distance to form a more complex network. You can also change to a heavier cord for a more sculptured effect. Finish the cording at one edge of the fabric.

8 Before sewing beads and barnacles, check that the hole or slot in your darning foot is large enough to fit around a raised bump of thread. Open darning feet are available for some machines, otherwise you may be able to modify the one you have. Some plastic darning feet have a small slot that can be enlarged by filing out the front of the foot. Some metal feet can also be adapted by filing out the front of the shape. Make sure the edges of the foot are very smooth so that they don't catch on the fabric. Resist the temptation to sew without a foot, as it is very difficult to avoid hitting the hard bump of thread, and you may break your needle. For the beads and barnacles, attach the open darning foot and follow the machine setting given in step 5. Use a beige or ochre thread on top and a

neutral-coloured thread in the bobbin. Bring up the bobbin thread as before and anchor the threads. If possible, move your needle position to far left. Change the stitch width to maximum (keep it to 5 if your machine does a very wide zigzag). Now, this is one technique where you must sew both *slowly and carefully*. Hold the fabric very still, and zigzag into the same two holes for about 15 stitches. Stop stitching. This makes a raised 'bead' of thread.

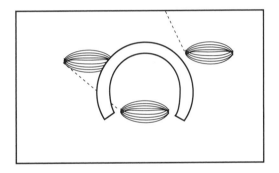

9 Turn the fabric 90° and stitch another 'bead' at right angles over the top of the first one. While stitching *very slowly*, rotate the fabric *very slowly* so the needle zigzags over the raised pile of thread, without letting the needle hit the bump, which would

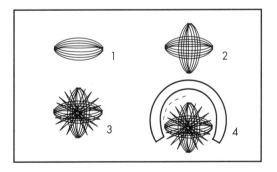

break it. Continue moving around the barnacle slowly until you have created a round raised bump.

10 Change the stitch width back to zero, which swings the needle over to the far left position, avoiding the barnacle. (If your machine is unable to do this, move the fabric slightly so that the needle stitches just on the edge of the barnacle.) A few short straight stitches will anchor the threads.

11 To move to the next place for another barnacle, you may sew backwards with straight stitch (easier with an open foot) or cut the threads and begin again. Work several barnacles around the lines created by the couching.

12 Smaller 'beads' can be sewn near the barnacles by following the first step in step 8. Don't sew over the top of the couched cords, as they will be too thick.

13 Place the completed embroidery face down on a thick bathtowel. Iron from the wrong side, using steam.

ARUM LILIES – HIGH RELIEF FLOWER PANEL

Many of my framed artworks include intensively stitched leaves, worked on a background of fine nylon tricot. This creates a firm yet flexible satiny fabric which is ideal for three-dimensional shapes. After finishing a particularly intensive piece in vivid colours inspired by tropical vegetation I saw in the Cairns botanical gardens, I decided to return to a pastel colour scheme and try some similar techniques for flowers.

The project explained here uses the arum lily, which has an elegant floral shape that can be made from one piece of embroidery rolled up and folded around a central stem. Lightweight iron-on interfacing is bonded over the back of the flower, adding extra body and covering the wrong side of the stitching. The flowers in the picture on page 96 are attached to a background, but similar smaller shapes would be effective wired and used in a spray, like the one shown on page 95 and explained on pages 81–4. Florists have arum lilies in many different varieties, so you may like to buy one or two of the flowers, and study the colours and sizes of the petals. The leaves are also beautiful, especially the ones in gorgeous variegated colours.

MATERIALS

Sheer knitted nylon fabric, in a colour to tone with embroidery threads
Backing fabric fused to heavyweight iron-on interfacing or cotton buckram
Scraps of white non-woven iron-on lightweight interfacing
Machine embroidery threads, and Bobbinfil or superfine overlock thread for the bobbin
Machine needle, size 90, Metafil
Darning foot
Satin-stitch foot
Machine embroidery hoop
Fabric marking pen
Scraps of coloured wool fibres or felt, for centre spike
Florists' wire, medium and fine gauge
Green florists' tape
Fabric glue
Candle supported in a candle holder

METHOD

1. Make a paper pattern for tracing the flower shapes. The largest one in the picture measures 12 cm (4³/4 in.) wide x 10 cm (4 in.) high. The leaf shape is 14 cm (5¹/2 in.) long x 6 cm (2¹/2 in.) wide. If you prefer, trace the

shapes of some real arum lilies and leaves. Stretch the nylon fabric very tightly in the embroidery hoop. Place the hoopful of fabric over the pattern for the flower, and trace it onto the nylon with the fabric marking pen. Make sure you include the stitching direction lines as shown. These will show you which way to slant the stitches, so they radiate from the centre of the base.

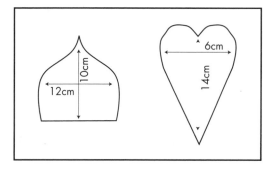

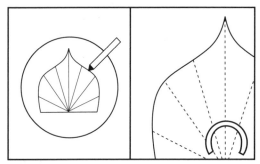

2   Thread the machine with the colour to be used on the outside edges of the flower, and put a toning colour in the bobbin. Attach the darning foot and lower or cover the feed teeth. Set the stitch length and width to zero, and loosen the tension slightly. Bring up the bobbin thread through the fabric and attach the threads. Outline the

tracing with straight stitch, including the stitching direction lines, running the machine fairly fast and moving the hoop smoothly.

3   Change the stitch width to 5 mm (1/4 in.) and turn the hoop so that the direction line at the base of the flower is lying across the centre of the darning foot. While running the machine at close to maximum speed, move the hoop slowly from side to side, in an east–west direction, moving from the edge of the flower to about halfway to the centre.

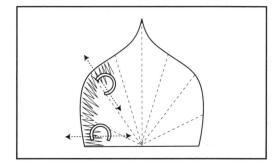

4   It is important to keep the stitching lying parallel to the directional lines, so when you progress a little further up the side of the flower, the next directional line will be at a slightly different angle, so move the hoop until it is again aligned across the centre of the foot, as shown above. Make the stitching dense enough to cover the background towards the outside edge, and a little more open towards the centre, as you will be overlapping with the second colour, which will fill in any spaces. Continue

Above: *Cushion cover with simulated smocking* (page 51) *and flower spray* (page 81)

Above: *Arum lilies* (page 93)

Above: *Dandelions* (page 60)

Above: *Backwards and forwards* (page 41)

Above: *Detail of dandelions* (page 60)

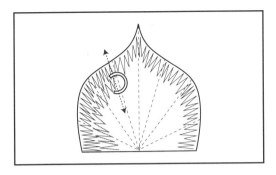

teeth, and set the stitch width to 5 mm ($^1/_5$ in.), and the stitch length to very close (or 0.5) for satin stitch. Beginning at the bottom of one side of the flower, satin stitch around the outside edge, slightly overlapping the edge of the thread painting. Taper the stitch width at the point at the top of the flower. This makes a neat firm edge when the flower is cut out. Don't sew across the base of the flower, as it makes it too bulky when it is gathered onto the stem.

moving around the edge of the flower, using this thread painting technique to fill the outer half of the flower shape. All the stitch lines should be slanting in towards the centre. Finish with a few straight stitches to end off the threads.

5 Change to the second colour and anchor the thread. Proceed in the same manner around the flower shape again, but this time overlapping the second colour into the spaces left at the edge of the first colour, and leaving the inside edge a little more open so you can overlap and blend in the third colour. As you will be thread painting in a smaller space, you will need to turn the hoop a little more to keep the stitches lying in the right direction.

6 End off the second colour with a few straight stitches, and attach the thread for the third colour. As this covers quite a small area, you will have to slant your stitches towards the central point, but don't make the area in the centre too thick or it may break your needle.

7 Rethread the machine with the first colour and attach the satin-stitch foot. Raise or uncover the feed

8 For an *optional* more natural looking edge, use the darning foot to sew a narrow line of thread painting around the inside edge of the satin stitching, blending the edge into the thread painting. However, be warned, this requires precise control of the hoop so that you don't overlap the outside edge, which would make it difficult to cut out without snipping a thread. If this step terrifies you, leave it out until you feel more proficient.

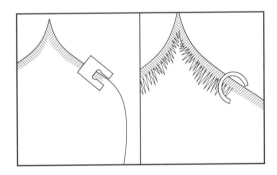

9 Hold the hoop of fabric up to the light to check for any missed areas or thin spots, and restitch if required. The stitches should cover the

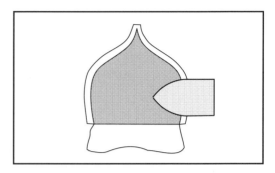

area smoothly, with no obvious gaps. However, it is not necessary to make the embroidery extremely dense, as this makes the flower very stiff. Remove the fabric from the hoop and use small sharp scissors to cut around the side of the flower, and also across the base, about 2 cm (³/4 in.) past the edge of the embroidery as shown below. This will leave you some soft fabric, which makes it easier to attach the flower to the wire.

10 Place the candle in a secure holder in a draught-free place, preferably with the light behind it (e.g. in front of a closed window). This makes it easier to see the edge as it melts. Hold the satin-stitched edge of the flower about 10 cm (4 in.) above the flame, so any shreds of nylon on the cut edge will be melted away. Be careful with pale colours as they may scorch if you hold them too close to the flame. Do not melt the extra fabric left at the base.

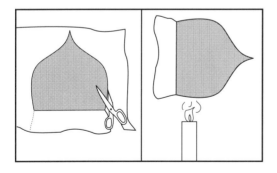

11 Trace the flower shape onto very lightweight iron-on interfacing, and cut out the interfacing about 2 mm (¹/8 in.) inside the tracing line. Place the interfacing glue-side down on the back of the flower and trim any edges that overlap the embroidered shape. (The intensive embroidery may have contracted the shape slightly.) Use a medium hot steam iron and a pressing cloth to fuse the interfacing to the back of the flower.

12 Take a medium gauge piece of florists' wire, and bend over 2 cm (³/4 in.) at one end. Fabric glue a tightly rolled scrap of wool or felt over this to make the spike for the centre of the flower. (The one in the picture on page 96 is about 1 cm (¹/2 in.) wide and 10 cm (4 in.) long.) Lay this over the centre of the flower, and fold and roll both sides over the middle at the base, securing all tightly with several wraps of fine wire, just at the base of the stitching

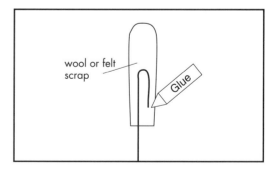

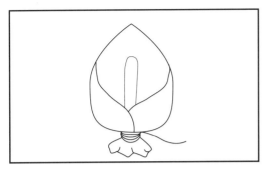

where it meets the extra unstitched fabric.

13 Cut 20 cm (8 in.) of florists' tape and wind firmly around the base of the flower, stretching tape slightly so it will cling, covering the wire and the excess fabric. Hold the flower in your right hand, and the tape and the wire in the left, stretching the tape slightly, turning the stem and smoothing the tape as it winds on.

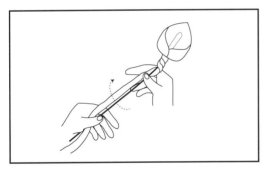

14 Spread open the base of the flower so it curves open attractively. Make several flowers, in a variety of sizes.

15 To make the leaves, trace a pattern on the nylon in the same way as for the flower. Proceed to stitch in the same way, following the direction lines, as described in earlier points. However, use the same colour in the bobbin as in the needle, as the leaves may be seen from both sides. Shade the colours used for the leaves from light in the centre to dark at the edges, and finish with satin stitch around the outside edge. Stitch a narrow line of satin stitch down the centre of the leaf.

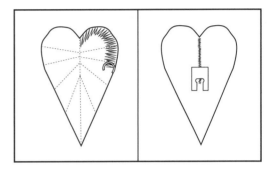

16 The flowers in the picture are attached to a background of fabric stiffened with firm iron-on interfacing. Use a small amount of fabric glue behind the base of the flower or the top of the leaf stem to attach them to the background. Pin the flowers to the base to hold the arrangement in place on a flat surface while the glue dries. Allow the leaves to fall forwards naturally to cover some of the stems. Alternatively, the leaves and flowers may be held in place by a small inconspicuous straight stitch using the zigzag foot.

MINCED FABRIC COCKTAIL HAT

I remember reading somewhere about an extremely well-organised lady who stored all her fabrics in neatly labelled boxes. One box contained 'pieces too small to be used'. If only she knew about minced fabric.

This is a technique I've often demonstrated to classes in residential workshops. Somehow, sitting in a group chatting, laughing and snipping is a therapeutic exercise, and the free-wheeling approach to colour and design is a good way to begin experimenting with colour mixing. The project I've shown (pictured on page 62) is an all-over blend of colours, but it is possible to create some extremely detailed works, reminiscent of Impressionist paintings.

Minced fabric can be used to create larger pieces for garments; smaller pieces for artworks or accessories; or to create individual accent areas within a larger work, such as the magnificent 'Ningaloo Reef' quilt, hand painted, printed and embroidered by Western Australian artist, Wendy Lugg.

Any kind of soft fabric works well for mincing, but try to select fabrics that are coloured on both sides. Thick fabrics are more difficult to use, as they may disintegrate into lots of fluffy pile if they are cut too small. I have used cotton buckram because the hat requires a stiff background. However, for a garment needing more flexibility, preshrunk iron-on woven interfacing works well.

MATERIALS

30 cm (12 in.) cotton buckram
30 cm (12 in.) paper-backed fusible webbing
30 cm (12 in.) lining fabric, e.g. taffeta
Scraps of soft fabric, coloured on both sides
Mylar Glitz threads or unravelled metallic threads
Fine net or tulle in a colour to tone with fabric scraps (fine black tulle is almost invisible over most bright colours)
Machine needle, size 90
Machine threads and embroidery threads
Zigzag foot
Satin-stitch foot
Darning foot
Rotary cutter and cutting board, or large sharp scissors
Fabric marking pen
Compass
8 m (8 3/4 yd) silky yarn or knitted rayon ribbon for tassel

METHOD

1 Draw a paper pattern for the hat. You will need a straight strip, approximately 10 cm x 60 cm (4 in. x 24 in.). (Measure the circumference of your head and add 2–3 cm ($3/4$–$1 1/4$ in.) for seams.) You will also need a circle to fit the top of the hat. The one in the picture was 20 cm (8 in.) in diameter, including seam allowances.

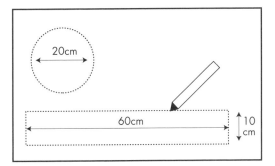

2 Trace the paper patterns onto the buckram and the paper-backed fusible webbing and cut out. Place the fusible webbing glue-side down on the buckram and iron over the paper backing with a fairly hot iron until fused. Set aside and peel off backing paper when ready to use.

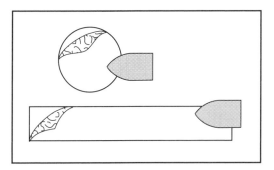

3 Close doors and windows, and turn off fans, as draughts will blow fabric fibres everywhere. Place the fabric scraps of similar colour together on the cutting board and roll the rotary cutter backwards and forwards over them, chopping them into small 1 cm ($1/2$ in.) pieces. Repeat for each colour, keeping each pile of minced fabric separate. If you are using scissors, cut the fabric into strips, then chop through several strips together to form small pieces. If you are doing this as a class exercise, each group could make several piles of different colours, and arrange these on a large table like a giant palette of colour for general use.

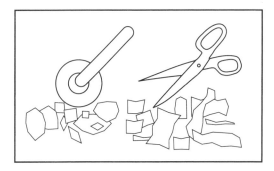

4 Peel the backing paper from the buckram, and lay the strip and the circle on the ironing board, glue-side up. Sprinkle the fabric scraps over the buckram, arranging the colours in your chosen design — lines, swirls, stripes or random mixtures. Make sure all of the backing fabric is covered with a layer of scraps. Don't make it too thick or the needle may break sewing through so many layers. For added excitement, sprinkle a few Mylar Glitz threads over the top.

5 Cover with a layer of baking paper and iron with a fairly hot iron until fused. Remove the baking paper carefully, and check for any missed areas, covering them with small snips of fabric. Not all the fabric scraps will have fused completely, only those in direct contact with the glue. However, if you are gentle with the fabric and don't shake it around too much everything will hold together until it is stitched.

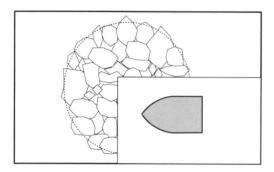

6 Cover the scraps with a layer of tulle and pin around the edges of the pattern pieces to prevent stray scraps escaping as you begin to sew. Thread the machine top and bobbin with a colour to tone with the fabric scraps. Attach the zigzag foot. Set the machine length and width to either a medium length straight stitch or a narrow width serpentine stitch. For the band, sew several undulating rows down the length of the strip. For the circles, begin in the middle and sew in a spiral movement towards the outside edge. This will prevent the scraps from moving.

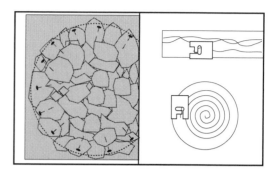

7 To decorate the surface, you can be as adventurous as you like. The hat in the picture has rows of undulating tapered satin stitch in several colours. You could also use automatic pattern stitches, or use a couching foot to attach cord or braid, or appliqué additional shapes on top of the minced fabric.

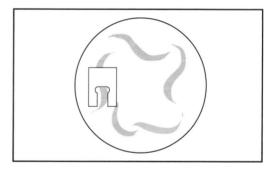

8 To make the little gold 'stamens', attach the darning foot, and lower or cover the feed teeth. Thread the needle with metallic gold thread, and put a colour to tone with the fabric scraps in the bobbin. If possible, set the needle position to far left, and set the stitch length and width to zero. Loosen the top tension by several degrees so the fine metallic thread does not break.

Bring the bobbin thread to the top of the fabric and anchor the threads. Move the fabric to the left to sew a line of straight stitch for the stem of the stamen, then hold the fabric still. Change the stitch width to 5 mm (¼ in.) and sew several zigzag stitches on the same spot, to build up a 'bead' of thread.

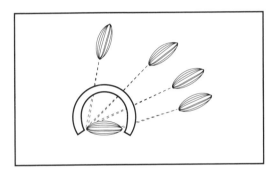

9 Change the stitch width back to zero. The needle will swing to the left and avoid the hard pile of thread that could break your needle. If this is not possible on your machine, move the fabric slightly, so the needle enters the fabric to the left of the bead. Sew back to the beginning of the stamen and repeat, moving the fabric slightly to sew the next stamen radiating out from the same central point. Sew bunches of stamens along the centre of the strip of fabric and around the circle, staying at least 2 cm (¾ in.) away from edges or seam allowances.

10 For the round 'barnacles' at the base of the bunch of stamens, sew a bead as explained in steps 8 and 9. Turn the fabric 90° and sew a second bead across the first one. While sewing *very slowly*, turn the fabric while zigzagging over the top of the pile of thread, building up a round bump of thread. Take care not to sew into the barnacle as it will break the needle. (See notes on modifying your darning foot, if necessary, on page 91.)

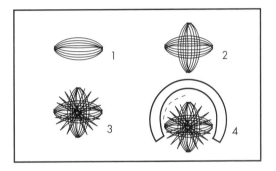

11 To complete the barnacle, change the stitch width back to zero, and sew a few straight stitches at the side of the barnacle to anchor the threads. Clip off the threads or sew straight stitch to the position for the next barnacle.

12 To make up the hat, press embroidery from the wrong side. Cut a strip and circle of lining fabric to match the embroidered pieces. Cut a circle of paper-backed fusible webbing to match the circle and fuse to the wrong side of the embroidery. Remove the paper, and cover the glue with the circle of lining fabric. Iron until fused.

13 To join the hat band to its lining, pin with right sides together. Sew a narrow seam along one of the long sides, using the zigzag foot and straight stitch. (Remember to raise or uncover the feed teeth and reset the stitch length

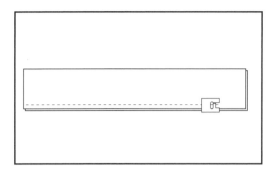

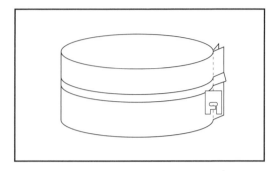

and tension after making the barnacles.) Open out and iron the seam towards the lining, then turn up a 1 cm (1/2 in.) hem on the embroidery to the inside, and press in place.

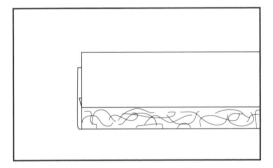

14 To check the fit of the hat band, fold into a circle and pin to fit the head as shown below. Open out the strip and sew a joining seam through the embroidery and the lining. Trim and

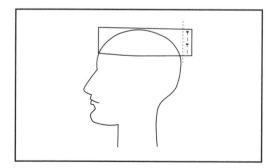

press the seam open, and press hem back along earlier fold line. Pin the hem and sew one or more lines of decorative stitching along the edge close to the fold, avoiding beads and barnacles. Pin along the open edge and trim the lining even with the embroidered fabric.

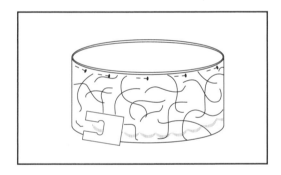

15 Check the fit of the circle to the band of the hat. The circle should be approximately 1–2 cm (1/2–3/4 in.) larger in diameter. Make small 5 mm (1/4 in.) snips all around the edge of the circle so that it will fit neatly when you pin it, right sides together, to the raw edge of the band. Mark the edge of the circle and the band into quarters and match these marks when you join the two pieces. This will be easier if you turn the band wrong side out, and place

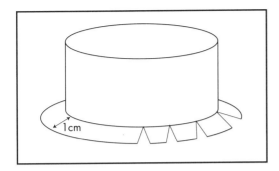

the pins at right angles to the edge as shown below. Pin and ease the circle into place, then stitch a 1 cm ($1/2$ in.) seam, working with the circle side on top, making sure to enclose all the snipped edges. Trim the seam neatly, and cover the raw edge of the seam with a narrow zigzag. Turn right side out.

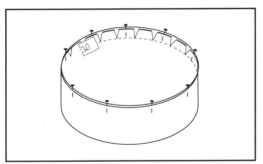

16 To make the tassel, wrap the knitted rayon ribbon or yarn around a piece of cardboard approximately 30 cm (12 in.) wide. Tie the two ends together, then tie through the centre of the bundle of strands to hold them together.

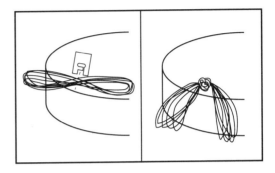

17 Fold the bundle in half, with the tied section in the centre. Place in position on the top of the hat, and sew straight stitch, forwards and backwards, across the centre of all the strands. Trim ends and threads. Tie both sides of the bundle in a single knot, covering the stitching.

BLUE BUTTERFLY WING CUTWORK YOKE

Sheer nylon knitted fabric or tricot is the most wonderfully versatile, inexpensive embroidery material to work on. It remains soft and supple even after intensive embroidery, and is ideal for cutwork (as in this piece pictured on page 43) because it does not fray. The excess tricot can be cut away, leaving a neat edge. Any small remaining wisps of fabric can be melted off by holding the edge above a candle flame.

Elaborate embroideries for garments or artworks are easily made using this method. Several smaller pieces can be joined invisibly by overlapping the nylon tricot, then embroidering over the join. This makes it possible to create fitted garments, with tucks and darts providing the shaping, which is then concealed by stitching.

Silky machine embroidery thread gives a luxurious satin surface, standard machine thread gives a firmer, matt finish. This technique is an exciting way to use the extensive colour range of machine embroidery threads now available. If you are hesitant about beginning your design, plan your piece first using coloured pencils, then trace the design onto tricot, indicating directions of stitching.

MATERIALS

Sheer nylon knitted fabric, in a colour to tone with embroidery threads
Machine embroidery threads
Fine good-quality overlock thread or Bobbinfil thread for the bobbin
Machine needle, size 90, with large eye
Free embroidery or darning foot
Satin-stitch foot
Wooden machine embroidery hoop, 23 cm (9 in.) size
Candle supported in a candle holder
Fabric marking pen or pencil
Snap-blade knife
Small spring clips to secure rolled-up fabric

METHOD

1 Inspiration for pattern shapes may come from a standard patten piece, e.g, a yoke or sleeve. You may wish to vary the shaping of the edges, e.g. hems or neckline, for a more exciting result. Cut a paper pattern and place on your body or pin to the garment to check the shape. Experimenting with coloured pencils on a pattern traced onto drawing paper is a good way to see how the finished design will look. The design in the picture on page 43 uses several shades of blue, green and turquoise, which flow from light to dark in a random pattern. The holes can be either small round ones or long sinuous curves, which are actually a row of small holes placed close together and separated by small narrow embroidered bars. The inspiration was taken from the wing of a tropical butterfly.

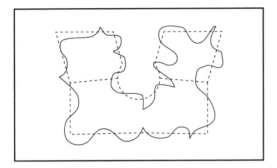

2 When you have chosen your pattern, spread the nylon over the top and pin at the corners to prevent it slipping while tracing. Trace the pattern, noting areas to be cut away for holes, and also indicating any important directions for shading or stitching. Try to have the stitching finishing at right angles to a hole or the edge of the embroidery. Remember to leave at least 5 cm (2 in.) extra fabric around the edge of the tracing so it can be easily stretched in the hoop.

3 Stretch the fabric in the embroidery hoop, beginning in the centre of the piece and working towards the edges. Roll up any excess fabric around the hoop and secure with small spring clips. Make sure the fabric

is firm and smooth. Thread the machine with the first colour, and put a toning shade (or one matching the nylon) in the bobbin. The example in the picture uses black nylon and matching bobbin thread. Attach the darning foot, and set the stitch length and width to zero. Lower or cover the feed teeth.

4 Bring the bobbin thread up through the fabric and anchor it. Cut off the thread ends. Begin by outlining the design with straight stitch. Run the machine fairly fast and move the hoop smoothly. Complete the area inside the hoop, and then move to another area, until the whole design has been traced in straight stitching. This thread tracing is more durable than fabric pen, which may disappear with much handling.

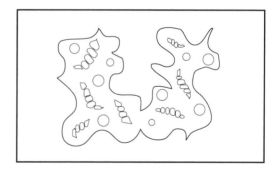

5 To colour the design, begin again in the centre of the piece. Anchor the threads as before, then change the stitch width to 5 mm (^{1}/4 in.) Don't exceed this width as the stitches will become too long and loopy. Run the machine fast and move the hoop in an east–west direction so that the stitches

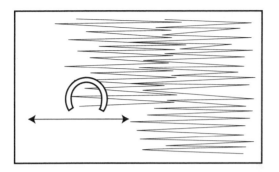

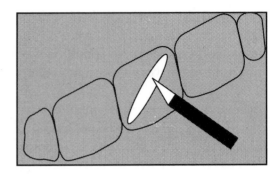

lie smoothly, forming a flat, satiny surface with no obvious ridges or lines.

6 To shade into the next area of colour, make the stitching at the edge of the colour area a little more open, leaving room for the next colour to be blended in. Begin and end each new colour with a few short straight stitches to anchor the threads. Complete the area in the hoop fully, both holes and thread painting, before moving to a new area.

7 To create the holes, the area to be cut away should be outlined with straight stitching as shown below. (This controls the size of the hole, which would otherwise spread out much further.) Keep the size of the hole to 1–2 cm ($1/2$–$3/4$ in.) maximum in diameter. Smaller holes are easier to deal with than larger ones. Cut and sew only one hole at a time, as this will help to keep the fabric firm and taut. Position the darning foot at the top of the first hole. Anchor the threads. Set the stitch width to maximum. With the snap-blade knife, cut a small vertical slit inside the longest axis of the first shape, about three-quarters of the length. Sew around the

slit, moving the hoop so that the foot follows the line of the straight stitching. The soft tricot will be rolled and stitched around the edge with an open zigzag, forming a neat hole. If you miss a little of the edge or the hole is not neat, repeat this last step. Move the hoop down and up as shown, so most of the stitches are lying at right angles to the edge. Don't turn the hoop round like a steering wheel; keep your hands flat on the side of the hoop and move down, slightly out, and up again. Move the hoop fairly quickly while running the machine at a medium speed, so the stitching around the edge forms an open zigzag rather than a close satin stitch, which would be too bulky. Finish stitching at the top of the next hole, and repeat the process until all the holes are stitched. Don't try

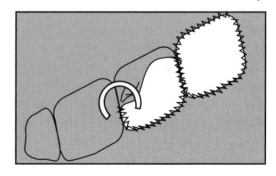

to make each hole very neat at this stage, as this is easier to do with the thread painting technique used later.

8 If you have several holes close together in a row, neaten the lines of stitching between each hole by moving slowly down the narrow bar formed by the rolled-up fabric, zig-zagging over the bar with the stitching at right angles to the bar.

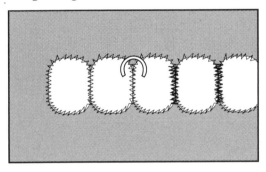

9 Continue filling in the solid areas with coloured stitching as in step 5. For the neatest edge where the thread painting meets the edge of a row of holes, slant the stitches so that they lie at right angles to the edge as shown below. For a larger hole, slant the stitches so that they radiate out from the central hole. When the area inside the hoop is filled, reposition it and continue sewing.

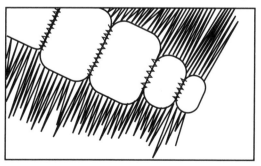

10 To finish the outside edge of the shape, attach the satin-stitch foot, and raise or uncover the feed teeth. Set the stitch width to 5 mm ($1/4$ in.) and the stitch length to very close or 0.5. Satin stitch around the edge of the piece, matching the colour of the thread to the completed embroidery. Taper the width of the satin stitch at points. Finish with a few short straight stitches.

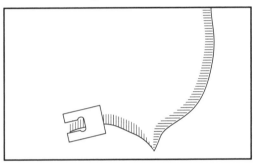

11 Use small sharp scissors to cut away the excess tricot, being careful not to snip the stitching. (Keep a bottle of clear nail polish nearby to dab on any errors to stop them unravelling.)

12 Set the candle on a firm base in a draught-free area, preferably with the light behind it (e.g. in front of a closed window). Hold the edge of the embroidery about 10 cm (4 in.) above the top of the candle flame, so that you can see any shreds of nylon melting in the heat. Be careful with very pale colours which may show a scorch mark if you hold the fabric too close to the flame. Note that the nylon melts easily, but if you are using an alternative backing fabric, be sure to do a sample

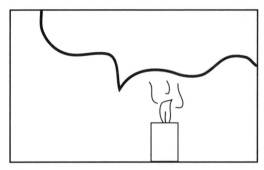

test first on a scrap as some fabrics flare and burn.

13 To join pieces, overlap them slightly at the edges, and pin in place while you check the fit and make any adjustments necessary. Stitch through both thicknesses using the zigzag foot and a straight stitch, and choosing a toning colour. Sew just inside the satin-stitched edge, so the stitches blend inconspicuously.

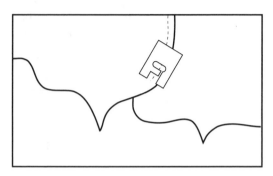

GLOSSARY

Appliqué Additional fabric sewn onto the surface for decoration.

Appliqué mat or pad Teflon-coated sheet used to prevent iron sticking to fusible fabrics. Baking paper may be used instead.

Automatic pattern stitches Repeating patterns formed by the machine setting the width, length etc. to create a continuous pattern. May be made completely automatically by pressing a single button, or by using the stitch selection dials or cams (plastic inserts which change the width and length of the stitch as they rotate). Modern electronic machines also have a memory facility which allows you to select and program your own patterns.

Backing fabric Fabric on which the embroidery or appliqué is sewn.

Baking paper Non-stick paper used to line baking trays (sheets) and cake pans. Ideal for use in embroidery, as glues and fusible fabric will not stick to it.

Bias Line crossing warp and weft threads at an angle of 45° to the straight grain.

Blind hem foot Sewing machine foot designed to be used with automatic blind hemstitch, which sews several straight stitches on edge of fabric, then does one zigzag stitch onto folded hem, so that only very small spaced stitches will be visible on outside of garment. As the foot is designed with a metal guide to position it close to the fabric edge, it can also be used with different needle positions for very close accurate edge stitching.

Blurring The technique of sewing along the edge of an appliqué fabric to cover the raw edge with several rows of straight or decorative stitching which blend the edge into the background. Best results are achieved with thread colours similar to either the appliqué fabric or the background fabric.

Bobbinfil Superfine white polyester thread made by Madeira to be used in the bobbin when sewing with fine machine embroidery threads. Useful because very fine gauge means that considerably more thread can be wound onto the bobbin than with normal threads, and this prevents thick build-up of thread on underside of intensively stitched work.

Buckram Close, even-weave cotton fabric, heavily stiffened with starch. Useful as a firm backing for embroidered artwork and as a stiffening for bags, belts and jewellery. Specify *cotton* buckram when purchasing, as other varieties are too heavy and stiff for machine embroidery. Clean machine frequently when using buckram as powdery starch collects under needle plate.

Cording needle Needle with a large eye made to take cordonnet (a thick thread used for decorative topstitching). Can also be used for machine-embroidery threads to prevent shredding and fraying. Also called a METAFIL NEEDLE or EMBROIDERY NEEDLE.

Couching Attaching a heavy yarn, cord or thread to the surface of the fabric with stitching. Sometimes called braiding.

Couching or braiding foot Machine foot

suitable for attaching cord or braid to the surface of fabric. Usually has one or more holes to thread the cord through, and a channel or groove underneath to allow the foot to move easily over the couching. Various types are available with different-sized holes to take fine to heavy cords. Multi-groove couching feet are also available with several grooves underneath to allow many cords to be attached simultaneously. These can be used with utility or decorative stitching.

Darning foot Machine foot suitable for free embroidery, i.e. sewing with the feed teeth disengaged (lowered or covered). Most models have a small spring which moves up and down with the needle so the foot holds the fabric down when the needle pierces it, thus making a stitch, and then moves up when the needle is out of the fabric, allowing you to move the fabric in any direction. Some models have a cut-out front, improving visibility. Darning feet are available for some machines with an extra large opening on the bottom to allow for easier work on thick fabric, e.g. quilting. Also called a FREE-EMBROIDERY FOOT.

Denim needles Machine needles with a longer, tapered point and a silicone coating made to penetrate easily through many layers of fabric or through heavy fabric. Suitable for embroidery on heavy fabric or for use with heavily layered or ruched fabric.

Embroidery foot *See* SATIN-STITCH FOOT.

Fabric marking pen Used for marking fabric before embroidery or cutting. Marks may be removed after use by sponging (the wash-out variety) or by exposing to light (the fade-out variety). Always test on scrap fabric before using.

Fabric paint Liquid paint suitable for applying to fabric. The kind that dries to a permanent waterproof finish and comes in a small bottle with a fine applicator nozzle is the easiest to use. Available in a wide range of matt, shiny and metallic colours.

Feed teeth or feed dogs Serrated metal teeth projecting through slots in the needle plate which move to draw fabric forwards or backwards under the needle. They should be lowered or covered for free machine embroidery.

Floating appliqué Embroidered pieces of fabric only partially attached to base fabric to create a three-dimensional effect such as leaves or flowers.

Florists' tape Trade name, Parafilm. Plastic tape used by florists to cover wire and stems of flowers. When stretched, it clings to wire. Available in several basic colours. A crêpe paper variety is also available.

Free arm The narrow, lower surface of the machine where sewing takes place. Made to allow small tubular areas of fabric, such as sleeves, trouser legs and cuffs, to be slipped over the arm so that they can be sewn more easily. Older machines do not have a free arm, but a flat, wide surface which is usually called a flat bed.

Free embroidery Embroidery done using a darning foot and with the feed teeth disengaged so that the fabric must be moved under the needle by hand. The base fabric should be stretched in a hoop, or stiff enough to move freely under the needle without wrinkling.

Hoop Two circles of wood, cane, metal or plastic that fit closely together to allow fabric to be tightly stretched for embroidery. Slim wooden hoops are the best quality. Spring-loaded plastic and metal hoops are useful for techniques where the hoop is repositioned often, e.g. lace-making on soluble fabric. However, they do not grip as tightly as a wooden hoop. Cane hoops are generally of poor quality. Wooden hoops grip better if the inner circle is wrapped with bias tape. The smaller the hoop, the tighter the tension possible on the fabric. Most wooden and plastic hoops have a screw or a spring to allow the tension on the outer hoop to be regulated.

Knee lift Knee-operated lever that raises and lowers presser foot, retracts feed teeth and reduces tension simultaneously, allowing both hands to be free to manipulate fabric. Available only on some models of Bernina machines.

Large-eyed needle Trade name Metafil. Also called a cording or cordonnet needle as the eye is large enough to take heavy thread. Used with a fine machine embroidery thread, it reduces splitting and shredding. The large eye makes it much easier to thread, and two threads can be used together to create a variegated or shaded effect.

Liquid fabric stiffener Clear, thickened liquid used to give a paper-like stiffness to limp fabric before embroidery. Apply to fabric, allow to dry and then iron before commencing embroidery. Rinses out in clear water after use. Easier and cleaner to use than starch.

Machine oil A fine quality oil used to lubricate some moving parts of the machine, e.g. hook race. Most machines require regular lubrication in this area. Be sure to buy the brand recommended by the machine manufacturer as some cheaper brands can become unpleasantly thick and sticky with age and damage the machine.

Machine embroidery threads Fine, glossy threads used for machine embroidery. Finer than standard sewing thread, and not strong enough for seams. Available in a large range of colours, plain, variegated and metallic. For best results, use with loosened top tension and a needle with a large eye.

Metafil needle See CORDING NEEDLE.

Muslin Fine, loosely woven, inexpensive cotton fabric similar to the gauze used for bandages. Can be used for a machine-sewn version of drawn threadwork.

Mylar threads Metallic or iridescent fibres used for appliqué, spinning and felting. Available in small packets and sold under the trade name Glitz.

Needle weaving Creating a woven type of fabric by stitching back and forth over a soluble fabric or over an open space. Similar to darning, although used decoratively.

Overlock thread A fine thread used in overlocking machines. The best quality superfine overlocking threads are also suitable to use in the bobbin when fine machine embroidery threads are used in the needle. Cheap, fuzzy overlock threads do not perform well and break frequently.

Paper-backed fusible webbing Fine, thread-like web of glue attached to non-stick paper. Use by placing the glue side down on fabric and ironing over the paper backing until the glue has melted, thus creating fabric with an adhesive backing. It is a versatile material for use with appliqué and embroidery. Trade name Vliesofix. Other brands do not perform as well, especially on cotton buckram.

Paint marker Marking pen filled with white oil-based paint. Available in fine, medium and bold point sizes. Useful for drawing on water-soluble fabric, where a water-based pen is not suitable.

Perspex insert Clear plastic tray made to fit around the free arm of the machine when it is being used in a sewing cabinet fitted with an automatic lift. The perspex extends the flat sewing surface around the foot, and the clear plastic allows easy vision of whatever is underneath, so the bobbin can be changed without removing the tray. A boon for sewers.

Pressing cloth A cotton cloth used over delicate fabric or embroidery when ironing to protect work from excessive heat or marking.

Rotary cutter Very sharp, circular cutting blade attached to handle, used with a rolling motion to cut multiple layers of fabric or paper. Safety cover slides up to cover blade when not in use. Must be used with a special plastic mat which is not damaged by cutting. Indispensable for patchworkers.

Rouleaux Narrow tubes of fabric made by cutting a strip of fabric on the bias, sewing it into a tube with a narrow seam and a close straight stitch, and turning it inside out. Because the fabric is cut on the bias, the tube is slightly stretchy when finished. A gadget called a rouleau or loop turner makes it easy to turn narrow tubes inside out. It is a long, thin piece of metal with a closed hook a little like a safety pin at one end and with a ring handle at the other.

Safety glasses Clear plastic glasses used to prevent eye injury when using fast-moving machinery, e.g. lathes, sewing machines. I have had an eye injury from a broken machine needle, and strongly recommend some kind of eye protection when using the sewing machine. Safety glasses are now available in many comfortable and attractive designs from hardware stores, optical dispensers and medical supply houses. Prescription glasses with large lenses also offer some degree of eye protection.

Satay stick A fine bamboo stick with a pointed end. Useful for manipulating or holding fabric as you sew — preventing stitched fingers.

Satin stitch Zigzag stitch sewn very close together, so stitches form a flat ribbon.

Satin-stitch foot Machine foot with a wide groove underneath to allow it to pass easily over raised areas of stitching such as satin stitch. Available in an open version which allows an uninterrupted view of the needle entering the fabric. Also called an EMBROIDERY FOOT.

Serpentine stitch Running stitch that curves from side to side in a regular wavy pattern. On some machines this is called a three-step zigzag as the pattern is more angular than wavy.

Shuttle The movable semicircular part that partially encloses the bobbin. It is designed with a pointed portion called the hook, which passes through the loop formed by the needle, thus forming the stitch. This area is not self-lubricating and should be kept oiled to keep the machine running smoothly and quietly.

Solvy Trade name in Australia for a cold-water soluble, plastic-like fabric.

Stabiliser Material used behind embroidery fabric when sewing to prevent it from puckering, stretching or tearing. Available in many different forms: permanent iron-on, removable iron-on, tear-away, wash-away (water-soluble). Different weights are available for different fabrics. In some cases, typing or computer paper can also be used. For very lightweight or delicate fabrics, use wash-away stabiliser or stretch the embroidery fabric in a hoop.

Stretch finger bandage A tubular elastic bandage useful for covering spools of slippery, silky machine embroidery thread to prevent unravelling. Available in several sizes. Choose a type with a good elastic content, as the knitted variety tends to lose its stretch.

Tension dial Device for regulating the pull of the thread through the needle or the bobbin. Many machine embroidery techniques require adjustment to the top and bobbin tension for different effects. Some bobbin cases (e.g. Bernina blacklatch bobbin case) are available with special tension adjustments for thick threads or loosened tension. A loosened top tension is generally advised when using machine embroidery or metallic threads, as these are not as strong as regular dressmaking threads.

Thread snips Small, spring-loaded scissors used by squeezing the outside of the plastic or metal covered blades. An indispensable tool, especially when worn on a ribbon around the neck that is just long enough to reach the machine foot for snipping threads.

Tricot Very fine, sheer, knitted synthetic fabric, often used to make lingerie. Usually available in pastel colours and sometimes in darker shades. This is a versatile fabric: it can be used as a backing for embroidery and is also good for cutwork and lace-making. Not widely available, but you can often find it in stores selling lingerie fabrics or in bargain stores with rolls of unusual fabric. Quite often very cheap, as its versatility is not widely known. Iron carefully as some nylon tricots have a low melting point.

Tulle Very fine net. It has a low melting point, so iron with care. Also called BRIDAL VEILING.

Twin needle/triple needle Double or triple needle attached to a single shank. Used for pintucking effects on fabric, where two or three top threads and one bobbin thread pull fabric up into a small ridge. May also be used with different coloured thread and pattern stitches. It is very important not to exceed the recommended width when using a twin or triple needle, or the needle will hit the foot or the needle plate and break. Never put the needle in the fabric before turning when using a twin or triple needle.

Twin needle button A button on some machines that regulates safe width for any patterns when using a twin needle.

Utility stitch Basic automatic stitches used for garment construction, seams, hems, on stretch fabrics, etc. Many of these can also be used decoratively.

Velcro Trade name for two-fabric strip system used for fastening. One strip has tiny, stiff plastic hooks which grip the other fuzzy strip. Available in several widths and colours.

Vilene Trade name in Australia and the United Kingdom (Pellon in the United States) for non-woven fabric used for backing or interfacing. Available in several weights from light to heavy, with or without iron-on fusible backing.

Vliesofix Trade name for paper-backed fusible webbing.

Walking foot Machine foot with feed teeth on top which work together with the lower feed teeth on the machine to draw fabric through evenly while stitching. Useful for sewing slippery or difficult fabrics like plastic, leather and rubber-backed curtain fabric, and ideal for machine quilting of several layers of fabric and batting (wadding). Also good for use with fabrics with stripes and patterns that must be matched precisely. If these are pinned first, the walking foot feeds them evenly so they do not slip out of alignment. Also called EVEN FEED FOOT.

Water-soluble fabric or stabiliser Trade name in Australia for cold-water soluble fabric is Solvy. Plastic-like fabric, available in varieties that are soluble in cold, hot or boiling water. Very versatile; can be used as a backing behind embroidery, as a base fabric for lacy embroidery (the base is washed away after stitching), as a top layer of fabric when sewing very fuzzy or hairy fabric which tangles around the machine foot, as a base fabric to support free shapes when doing cutwork, or as a support fabric to enclose threads or fabric scraps when creating fabric. You can now buy soluble laundry bags, originally made to hold contaminated linen in hospitals. At present these are only available in bulk quantities, but they are much cheaper, stronger and easier to use than the cold-water soluble fabric. These bags dissolve in hot water.

Zigzag foot Machine foot with a flat base and a rectangular slot for the needle. Suitable for straight or zigzag stitching.

LIST OF SUPPLIERS

This is a list of sources for some of the materials mentioned in the projects which may not be readily available in your area. Although some companies will only supply wholesale quantities, it is worth contacting them to find out whether there is a retail supplier in your area who may be able to get stock for you. Most suppliers have a mail order service, often with comprehensive catalogues or sample swatches available for a small fee. If you are a member of a textile group, you may be able to purchase the quantity required and divide it among interested members.

KIRSTEN YARNS PTY LTD
PO Box 197
Canterbury Vic. 3126
Ph. (03) 836 4385
Hand-dyed yarns, knitted rayon ribbon, exotic yarns.

TREE TOPS COLOUR HARMONIES
Nancy Ballesteros
6 Benwee Road
Floreat WA 6014
Ph. (09) 387 3007
Hand-dyed wool, silk, mohair tops, custom dyeing, Mylar Glitz fibres.

FILTER FAB LAUNDRY SUPPLIES
25 John Street
Mascot NSW 2020
Ph. (02) 667 1483
Hot-water soluble laundry bags (wholesale quantities).

PENGUIN THREADS PTY LTD
25–27 Izett Street
Prahran Vic. 3181
Ph. (03) 529 4400
Madeira machine embroidery threads, braids (wholesale quantities).

CHARLES PARSONS PTY LTD
Textile Distributors
100 Chalmers Street
Surry Hills NSW 2010
Ph. (02) 699 9444
Lightweight cotton buckram or stiffened cotton, sold as FormRite, item no. 160M. Heavier weight cotton buckram (wholesale quantities).

K MART AUSTRALIA
Sheer nylon tricot, sold as 'dress weight nylon'.